In tribute to the founding
Chairperson of independent sector

JOHN W. GARDNER

we are pleased to present you with
this book of inspiration in
recognition of your valuable service
to the nonprofit sector.

The San Francisco Host Committee
2003 Independent Sector Annual Conference

This gift sponsored by The James Irvine Foundation.

To the love of John W. Gardner's life
who shared the passage for sixty-seven years
AIDA MARROQUIN GARDNER
and to their family
all three generations

I speak for an optimism that does not assume it has found a cure for all of life's ills, that recognizes the deep, intrinsic difficulties in social change, that accepts life's often unfavorable odds—but will not stop hoping, or trying, or enjoying when it's possible to enjoy.

No doubt the world is, among other things, a vale of tears. It is full of absurdities that cannot be explained, evils that cannot be countenanced, injustices that cannot be excused. The individual who does not understand that is disarmed in a hazardous environment.

But then there is the resilience of the human spirit. Hope runs deeper than intellectual appraisal. We were designed for struggle, for survival. Only fatal and final injuries neutralize that irrepressible striving toward the light. Our conscious processes—the part of us that is saturated with words and ideas—may arrive at exceedingly gloomy appraisals, but an older, more deeply rooted, biologically and spiritually stubborn part of us continues to say yes to hoping, yes to striving, yes to life.

—Recovery of Confidence, 1970

Living, Leading, and the American Dream

John W. Gardner

edited by

Francesca Gardner

foreword by

Bill Moyers

Published with the support of the Ewing Marion Kauffman Foundation

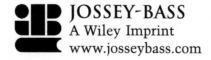

JOSSEY-BASS
A Wiley Imprint
www.josseybass.com

Published by Jossey-Bass
A Wiley Imprint
989 Market Street, San Francisco, CA 94103-1741   www.josseybass.com

Jossey-Bass books and products are available through most bookstores. To contact Jossey-
Bass directly call our Customer Care Department within the U.S. at 800-956-7739, outside
the U.S. at 317-572-3986 or fax 317-572-4002.

Jossey-Bass also publishes its books in a variety of electronic formats. Some content that
appears in print may not be available in electronic books.

Credits are located in the Notes section, pages 233–238.

Library of Congress Cataloging-in-Publication Data

Gardner, John William, date.
  Living, leading, and the American dream / John W. Gardner; edited by
Francesca Gardner; foreword by Bill Moyers; afterword by Brian
O'Connell.—1st ed.
    p. cm.
Includes bibliographical references and index.
  ISBN 0-7879-6678-9 (alk. paper)
  1. Political participation—United States. 2. Civil society—United
States. 3. Social values—United States. I. Gardner, Francesca, date.
I. Title.
  JK1764.G368 2003
  300'.973—dc21

                              2003005576

Printed in the United States of America
FIRST EDITION
HB Printing   10 9 8 7 6 5 4 3 2 1

CONTENTS

Foreword   xiii

Bill Moyers

Preface   xvii

About John W. Gardner   xxi

About the Editor   xxvii

PART ONE

A Life in Action—and Reflection

1 Glimpses of My Life   3

Looking back I see a California boy finding his way through life, endlessly challenged, surmounting obstacles, falling on his face, always studying, always trying, always wondering.

2 In the President's Cabinet   11

It was terribly important to respect the difficulty of the job, to respect the best people there, to respect the good parts of those who weren't the best, and to understand the system even if it was your intention to fight it.

3 Leading Common Cause 29

As citizens we have every right to raise hell when we see injustice done, or the public interest betrayed, or the public process corrupted.

PART TWO

The Courage to Live and Learn

4 Personal Renewal 41

Life isn't a game that has a score. Nor a riddle that has an answer. Life is an endless unfolding, and if we wish it to be, an endless process of self-discovery.

5 How to Tell When You've Grown Up 55

It takes much longer to grow up than one might imagine.

6 The Fourth Maxim 57

Live, Love, Learn . . .

7 Touch the Earth 61

Dig your fingers into the soil. Acknowledge your roots. Know where you came from and the earth that nourished you.

8 The Qualities of Creativity 65

People think of creativity as a kind of psychic wonder drug, powerful and presumably painless; everyone wants a prescription.

PART THREE

The Release of Human Possibilities

9 Commitment and Meaning   75

We have throughout history shown a compelling need
to arrive at conceptions of the universe in terms of
which we could regard our own lives as meaningful. We
want to know where we fit into the scheme of things.

10 Motivation and the Triumphant Expression
of Talent   85

Talent is one thing; its triumphant expression is quite
another. . . . The maturing of any complex talent requires a happy combination of motivation, character
and opportunity.

11 The Full Expression of Human Excellence   93

The question of excellence is only one of the many problems facing a free society. But it is a problem that cuts
across all the others.

12 Our Moral and Spiritual Lineage   103

No one can measure the contagion of ideas, values, and
aspirations as expressed in the lives and acts of individual men and women.

PART FOUR

Leading and Managing

13 The Nature of Leadership 113

The aura with which we tend to surround the words *leader* and *leadership* makes it hard to think clearly. Good sense calls for demystification.

14 The Tasks of Leadership 127

Any attempt to describe a social process as complex as leadership inevitably makes it seem more orderly than it is. Leadership is not tidy.

15 The Heart of Leadership 143

Executives are given subordinates; they have to earn followers.

PART FIVE

Renewing Our Society

16 The American Experiment 159

We are capable of so much that is not now asked of us. The courage and spirit are there, poorly hidden beneath self-interest and self-indulgence, waiting to be called forth.

17 Building Community 175

The process of renewal encompasses both continuity and change, reinterpreting tradition to meet new conditions, building a better future on an acknowledged heritage and the wisdom of experience.

18 Leading Community 195

Individuals at all levels of society must be prepared to exercise leaderlike initiative and responsibility.

19 The Independent Sector 205

Americans do not regard the furtherance of public purpose as a monopoly of government, and that belief has brought a great release of human energy.

20 The American Dream 213

My deepest admiration goes to those many Americans who are keeping the Dream alive today.

21 Freedom and Obligation, Liberty and Duty 219

When we raise our sights, strive for excellence, dedicate ourselves to the highest goals of our society, we are enrolling in an ancient and meaningful cause.

Afterword 229
Brian O'Connell

Notes 233

Index 239

FOREWORD

I met John Gardner in 1965 when I was very young and he was very wise. Over the years I never grew younger but he seemed always to grow wiser. He was remarkable in that respect. Scotty Reston, the *New York Times* chief in Washington, befriended both of us. "Take him as your mentor," Scotty told me, "and you will see how to live the greatest number of good hours."

It took me a while to grasp the full implication of that advice, but as we worked together—I as a White House assistant and John as Secretary of Health, Education, and Welfare—and as I read his books for insight and his life for instruction, I came to see what Scotty meant. Here was a man who "saw the present right" and marched to it, without conceit or self-deceit. Feeling the past and anticipating the future, he nonetheless lived in the meantime. The meantime, he believed, is our field of encounter, the hinge on which hope turns, the one chance we have for happiness, service, and meaning. So he was, in his own words, "always studying, always trying, always wondering." He built meaning into his life because there was no other way to achieve it. "Meaning doesn't come in the genes," he said; "You compose it. You compose it out of your own past, out of your affections and loyalties, out of the experience of humankind as it is passed on to you, out of your own talent and understanding, out of the things you believe in, out of the things and people you love, out of the values for which you are willing to sacrifice something. The ingredients are there," he said; "You are the only person who can put them together into the unique pattern that will be your life."

That's what John Gardner believed. That's what John Gardner taught. And that's what John Gardner did.

"He thinks like a saint," a White House aide once said of him. "No," said Lyndon Johnson, "he thinks like a good Republican. They're harder to find than saints. And besides, one is all you need."

They were the right two at the right time. Johnson—impetuous, imperious, impatient; Gardner—reflective, righteous, resolute. Both were radical middle-of-the-roaders who believed in widening the road into a broad boulevard of opportunity so more people could travel it.

One memorable summer evening, we sat on the south lawn of the White House—the six of us: LBJ and Lady Bird, John and Aida Gardner, Judith and me, both of us barely thirty. I just listened that evening, listened to one man who understood power and politics and another who understood process and programs. Equality was no stranger to their political discourse, and it was clear to me both intended a fair and just America. Lyndon Johnson knew how to create opportunity; John Gardner how to fulfill it. One night, after Sargent Shriver proved uncharacteristically slow in filling new regional positions created for the Office of Economic Opportunity, the President said to me: "If those regional poverty jobs are not filled this week, I'm going to take back the super grades and give them to John Gardner for the Office of Education." I wrote Shriver with the message and no sooner was the letter read than the jobs were filled; no one doubted Gardner would have grabbed them up in one fell swoop. Joe Califano remembers LBJ telling him, "If Gardner doesn't slow down spending [on hospital construction], we'll have another 1929." No wonder his department got more than one hundred pieces of legislation through Congress, or that he was soon supervising programs that affected 195 million Americans.

Sadly, their collaboration and aspirations were orphaned by war. On the very next day after announcing that he was sending ground troops to Vietnam, the President stood in the Rose Garden to announce he was appointing John Gardner to head of HEW. Whatever happens in Vietnam, the president said, we'll not fail to pursue the Great Society. That was so for a while. But two years later, John went to the LBJ ranch in Texas to plead for larger appropriations for Health, Education, and Welfare. The president had to turn him down and cut even more from the budget as it was. Gardner responded with a muted anguish that pained the President. As he was about to get out of the car, LBJ put his arm around him and said, "Don't worry, John. We're going to end this damned war and then you'll have all the money you want for education, and health, and everything else." It was not to be. Less than a year later John Gardner would tell the President in an emotional private meeting that he was resigning. "I believe you can no longer pull the country together," he said to LBJ. But in an election year "you deserve the total support of every cabinet member and a cabinet member who doesn't think you should run shouldn't be in the cabinet."

That's the kind of man this was. He gave up his position but not his principles or passion. And in the files of the LBJ library in Austin there is a letter from John to the library director, Harry Middleton, written in the late seventies and commenting on various critiques of the Great Society programs. John remained hopeful. "I see a society learning new ways as a baby learns to walk. He stands up, falls, stands again, falls and bumps his nose, cries, tries again—and eventually walks." Not in Gardner's America would anyone stick to crawling. The weakest would be helped to their feet; business might be all about the economics of competition, but to him our civic and political culture was about the ethos of cooperation. His greatest fear was that America would be a great nation full of talented people with enormous energy who forgot they needed each other.

It's been said he was a romantic. He had, after all, dropped out of Stanford intending to become a novelist until he tried writing a novel. But he had also been a Marine Corps captain during World War II, and marines are not easily duped by illusion. He knew the brokenness of things, but believed in wholeness. Civil rights, education, campaign finance reform, Medicare, public television, the White House fellows, Common Cause—all bore his mark, and his mark was all about healing.

I remember what he told us when he came to Washington in 1965: "What we have before us are some breathtaking opportunities disguised as insoluble problems." A man who knows that knows the score and is unafraid of it. I was fortunate to meet him so young and to know him so long. He taught me that the best way to live is to imagine a more confident future and wake up every day to do whatever one can to bring it about. Asked about his legacy, he replied that he would like it not to be another John Gardner but thousands of John Gardners—all working to improve the quality of life in America. Thanks to him, there are. Emerson, who was Scotty Reston's source, must have had the likes of John Gardner in mind when he wrote: "To finish the moment, to find the journey's end in every step of the road, to live the greatest number of good hours, is wisdom."

New York, New York
April 17, 2002

Bill Moyers
Eulogy for John Gardner

PREFACE

This book brings together selected writings of my father, John W. Gardner. In a lifetime that spanned the twentieth century, Gardner was a college teacher, military intelligence officer, foundation executive, author, cabinet secretary, founder of numerous organizations including Common Cause, INDEPENDENT SECTOR, and the White House Fellows, and champion of citizen participation and political reform. "He was," says Brian O'Connell, co-founder of INDEPENDENT SECTOR, "the dreamer who could teach, the teacher who could write, and the writer who could organize institutions and crusades to make shared dreams come true."

In the last years of his life, I was privileged to spend many hours with him reviewing his writings for a possible book. In addition to all of his published works, we went back through fifty years of essays, speeches, journals, and casual writings. This book grew out of that work, and is informed by our many discussions of what was most important and most interesting to him. Unfortunately, he did not live to see this volume completed. But his spirit is behind every decision.

Many of the pieces are published here for the first time. The mind of the writer was always at work. As he got ideas, he would write thoughts in journals for future reference. Later he might return to develop them more fully, and finally include them in a speech, essay, or book. Bits and pieces, conceived in the middle of other work, would evolve into fully formed concepts. Previously explored concepts would appear years later, fleshed out and expanded in light of new research or experiences. Journal entries became chapters—or organizations! Once I asked if it didn't bother him when someone appropriated an idea. His response was: "No, I have lots more ideas where that one came from."

OVERVIEW OF THE BOOK

For John W. Gardner, as the pieces collected in this book make clear again and again, healthy societies require healthy individuals—and vice versa. Those interested in the fulfillment of the individual, as Gardner was, need to work to improve the communities, organizations, and societies in which individuals live. Those interested in strengthening communities, organizations, and societies need to pay attention to the well-being of the individuals who compose them. In his writings, he constantly moved back and forth between the individual and society. For this book, however, the writings are organized according to whether they focus on the individual or on society.

Part One, A Life in Action—and Reflection, begins the book with three chapters about the life and times of the author. Chapter One provides glimpses into his private life. Chapter Two, published here for the first time, recalls his service as Secretary of Health, Education, and Welfare and key lessons he learned about leadership, power, and public service. In Chapter Three, he reflects on Common Cause, citizen action, and some stories of the efforts to make government more accountable.

Part Two, The Courage to Live and Learn, brings together some of Gardner's most popular articles and speeches on individual fulfillment. Chapter Four emphasizes the importance of continual learning and self-renewal. Chapter Five provides guidelines for assessing, with a measure of humor, one's own level of maturity. Chapter Six examines the power of a single word. Chapter Seven explains the value of being grounded in your own history even as you may attempt to escape it. And Chapter Eight describes characteristics of successful innovators.

In Part Three, The Release of Human Possibilities, Gardner provides insights into some of the deepest human yearnings and the interaction between the individual and society in responding to them: the universal quest for meaning and fulfillment in Chapter Nine, the release of human possibilities in Chapter Ten, the need for excellence in Chapter Eleven, and the search for values we can live by in Chapter Twelve.

Part Four, Leading and Managing, moves to the practical aspects of achieving important group purposes, with Chapter Thirteen's analysis of the nature of leadership in all its forms. Chapter Fourteen outlines the key tasks for effective leaders, and Chapter Fifteen discusses how successful leaders inspire, motivate, and activate followers.

Part Five, Renewing Our Society, focuses on the great social and political experiment that is America. In Chapter Sixteen the current state of the experiment and the challenges of our democratic society are discussed. In Chapter Seventeen, the subject is strengthening communities at the grass roots. In Chapter Eighteen, we move to the task of leading communities that are increasingly diverse; in Chapter Nineteen, to the important role of the independent sector in our society; and in Chapter Twenty, to one man's vision of the American Dream.

Chapter Twenty-One ends this book with a selection from *Excellence* and Gardner's concept of the pact that underlies a free society. "Freedom and obligation, liberty and duty—that's the deal. May we never forget it." John W. Gardner never did forget it.

A NOTE ON THE EDITING PROCESS

Because the text of this book includes pieces from many sources, the Endnotes specify the source for each chapter. The reader interested in reading more on a subject may wish to check some of these. Not all selections are presented exactly as they appear in the original source. My father and I thought it fair that the author be allowed to edit his own work so long as it was limited to changes in language without changing the idea being conveyed. I have used that same measure in changes made more recently. Such changes have often been made to adapt the length of a piece to the context of this book.

ACKNOWLEDGMENTS

Thanks go to Aida Gardner, Stephanie Trimble, Justine Reese, Jennifer Reese, John Gardner Trimble, and Bill Trimble for moral as well as editing support during the long gestation of this book; to Richard Van Wagenen and Tracy and Charles Stephenson for reviewing manuscripts with great care; to the Haas Public Service Center at Stanford University for assistance in smoothing the way to the finish; and to Dulce Carothers for her whole-hearted efforts and assistance to Dad and me at every stage of creation over many years. Special thanks to Brian O'Connell and the Ewing Marion Kauffman Foundation for the encouragement and support which provided the impetus to bring the project to completion, and to Alan Shrader for his steady, kind, and thoughtful help and advice as I completed this collaborative project without my original collaborator.

San Francisco, California   Francesca Gardner
March 2003

ABOUT JOHN W. GARDNER

John W. Gardner was a California native who grew up with all the sunny optimism that implies. He was born in Los Angeles on October 8, 1912. He spent his earliest years in what was then the tiny new village of Beverly Hills, where he played in the lima bean fields and watched movies being made in the streets. He visited Hawaii for extended periods of time, where he attended school, climbed the palm trees with local boys, and took swimming lessons from the legendary Duke Kahanamoku (the first Hawaiian Olympian and father of modern surfing). Summers in California's Gold Country, on the American River, included sleeping on a bed of pine boughs lashed to trees, fishing, hiking, hunting, and panning for gold under the supervision of his uncles, gold miners who had been to the Yukon. At age sixteen, in 1928, he took a trip around the world with his grandparents. It was a childhood full of change, variety, independence, and opportunities to grow and explore.

In 1929, Gardner entered Stanford University, beginning an association with that university that lasted for the rest of his life. He initially focused his energies on literature and competitive swimming: he broke several Pacific Coast intercollegiate swimming records but liked to emphasize that he achieved no comparable distinction in literature. He had always been a voracious reader and planned to become a novelist. His plan changed after he met and decided to marry Aida Marroquin. Doubting that he could support a family as an author, he shifted to the field of psychology and married in his senior year. He was awarded his B.A. "with great distinction" in 1935 and his M.A. in 1936 from Stanford. He received a Ph.D. from the University of California at Berkeley in 1938.

He immediately headed East with Aida and their first child, Stephanie, to teach psychology at Connecticut College and later at Mount Holyoke. His career as a psychologist was brief, but the grounding in psychology had a profound effect on his intellectual development: psychological concepts and insights are woven into virtually all of his writings.

By the time of Pearl Harbor, Gardner had concluded that college teaching was not for him. Against the counsel of colleagues ("You will never get tenure!"), he sought a wartime assignment in Washington, D.C. He spent a year with the Federal Communications Commission before entering the U.S. Marine Corps. As a marine, he was assigned to the Office of Strategic Services and sent to Italy and then Austria. For the first time in his life, he had to manage and lead. He had always seen himself as scholar, reader, and thinker and was surprised to find that he enjoyed the new roles. For the rest of his life, he moved between the life of action and the life of reflection with ease.

During the war, Gardner's focus, which had been on the individual, shifted to the broader forces that had so impacted the country and world. He began studying and thinking about public affairs, governance, and societal values. He started down a new path.

When the war ended, Gardner was offered a job with the Carnegie Corporation of New York, a major philanthropic foundation. He accepted readily, without inquiring about salary. When asked why the question of salary was not raised, he reportedly replied, "If I like the work, it won't matter. I'll stay. And if I don't like it, it won't matter because I'll leave." He stayed nineteen years, becoming president of the foundation after nine.

The job at Carnegie provided an opportunity to observe, over a broad range of fields, how ideas are translated—or fail to get translated—into action. As a foundation officer and later as a director of major corporations, a member of the Scientific Advisory Board of the Air Force, a trustee of the Metropolitan Museum of Art, and consultant to a half dozen federal agencies, he observed organizations large and small, and individuals at all levels, working in diverse settings, addressing a multiplicity of challenges, sometimes succeeding, sometimes not. He became very aware of the over-

About John W. Gardner

riding need for continuous attention to renewal—individual, organizational, and societal. He began to write again, but *not* fiction. The earliest pieces included in this collection are from two of his most popular books, *Excellence* and *Self-Renewal,* both written during that period.

Published in 1961, *Excellence: Can We Be Equal and Excellent Too?* touched on themes destined to reappear and evolve in his later work: motivation, fulfillment, renewal, values, shared purposes, leadership. The underlying theme then and throughout his work was how to facilitate the release of human possibilities—by motivating the individual, by creating a just society, by removing barriers to individual growth. "What we must reach for is a conception of perpetual self-discovery, perpetual reshaping to realize one's best self, to be the person one could be." The psychologist in him was never far away.

It was this book, much admired by President John F. Kennedy, that led Kennedy to put him on the list for the Presidential Medal of Freedom, the nation's highest civilian honor, which President Johnson awarded him in 1964. He was also enlisted as editor of *To Turn the Tide,* a selection of writings and speeches by Kennedy in his first year as president.

Excellence was followed three years later by *Self-Renewal,* which explored more comprehensively the themes of personal, social, and institutional renewal and the interplay between the individual and society. "Society is not like a machine that is created at some point in time and then maintained with a minimum of effort; a society is being continuously re-created, for good or ill, by its members. This will strike some as a burdensome responsibility, but it will summon others to greatness." These first two books found ready audiences, and have remained in print (in revised editions) ever since.

Gardner chaired President Lyndon B. Johnson's Task Force on Education (1964) and the White House Conference on Education (1965). In 1965, he accepted President Johnson's invitation to become Secretary of the Department of Health, Education, and Welfare. The move from the relatively tranquil environment of a foundation with a staff of thirty-six to a public agency with 105,000 employees was a tumultuous learning experience. For three years, he absorbed wholly new lessons about almost wholly new worlds. As he launched Medicare, undertook the first enforcement of the Civil Rights Act of 1964, and presided over the headiest days of Great Society legislation, he learned to deal with the media, cope with the complexities of Congress, and fight tough battles in the public forum. *No Easy Victories* (1968) came out of the experiences of these government years, giving new attention to issues of power and government functioning.

In 1968, Gardner left government service and became the first full-time chairman and CEO of the newly formed National Urban Coalition. The Coalition, an extraordinary group of leaders from all walks of American life, came together to tackle the problems of race and poverty that underlay the nationwide riots of the late 1960s. He took the post in March. It was a time of anger and disruption. Martin Luther King Jr. was assassinated in April and Robert Kennedy in June. The unrest and the breakdown of social cohesion led to Gardner's intense interest in the citizen's role in social change, his conviction that sustained citizen participation would be necessary to solve the problems ahead. His thoughts on this came to the fore in *The Recovery of Confidence* (1970) and led to his next major project, Common Cause.

Common Cause, founded in August 1970, was Gardner's response to the lack of a citizen advocacy group. "Everybody is represented but the people," he said. For seven years he led efforts to represent the people. A hundred thousand citizens joined Common Cause during the first twenty-three weeks of its existence. Concerned that they all understand fully what the movement was about, Gardner wrote night and day to produce *In Common Cause* (1972), a book on government power and citizen roles, with discussion on corruption, conflicts of interest, advocacy, accessibility, and responsiveness. His years in government and the Urban Coalition were rich resources for understanding these new topics.

In the midst of this active work, Gardner, who had always loved well-written words, coedited a book of favorite quotations from the vast collection he kept in multiple binders. It was a labor of love that became *Quotations of Wit and Wisdom,* a book totally different from his prior books, which has been in print for more than twenty-eight years.

About John W. Gardner

After leaving Common Cause in 1977, when he was sixty-five years old, Gardner wrote *Morale,* which addressed the earlier themes of motivation and morale in the context of his growing concern about governance and political possibility. These new interests led him to become a member of President Carter's Commission on an Agenda for the 80s, and of President Reagan's Task Force on Private Sector Initiatives.

About this time, he also embarked on a new venture. His ongoing involvement with the nonprofit sector in American life, which began in his foundation years, led him to join with Brian O'Connell in founding INDEPENDENT SECTOR in 1980. INDEPENDENT SECTOR became a forum for the whole range of nonprofit organizations. Gardner spent the next five years seeing the new organization through its formative period. It would take another decade for informed Americans to fully realize the crucial role of the nonprofit sector in our society—a role now widely discussed under such labels as "social capital" and "civil society."

Gardner then moved on to a more contemplative project—a study of leadership. All his prior work had involved continuous searching for effective leaders in both the public and private sector, for men and women capable of advancing group purpose. The Urban Coalition and Common Cause years particularly had focused his mind on the topic. For five years he devoted full time to research and study, a distinct change from the life of action he had led while doing his earlier writing. The product was *On Leadership,* published in 1990.

By the time *On Leadership* was published, Gardner had returned to California, where he taught leadership and organizational renewal at Stanford University's Graduate School of Business and then became a consulting professor in the School of Education. His work on leadership convinced him of the importance of understanding the social system in which leaders function. Recognizing that diminished social cohesion severely limits the leader's capacity to lead, he next revisited the issues of community that had occupied him as chairman of the National Urban Coalition in the late 1960s. His studies led to *Building Community* (1993, published in booklet form by INDEPENDENT SECTOR), and later to his accepting of the chairmanship of the National Civic League in 1994. Looking at cities all across the nation from this vantage point and finding an impressive wave of innovation in progress, he recorded his thoughts in *National Renewal* (1995, also published in booklet form by INDEPENDENT SECTOR).

At the time of his death in 2002, Gardner was immersed in yet another study, a deeper exploration of the attitudes, beliefs, and practices that can restore social wholeness to a community while incorporating diversity. *The American Experiment* was his last major essay. Reminding us that both Jefferson and Madison described our new nation as an experiment, Gardner says, "The experiment is still in progress." Americans in all their diversity are still engaged in it—they "are all working on the same quilt."

John Gardner died on February 16, 2002. He was eighty-nine years old. He worked till he could work no longer, writing, studying, communicating with colleagues, and thinking about the future of the nation.

About John W. Gardner

ABOUT THE EDITOR

Francesca Gardner grew up in Scarsdale, New York. She attended college and law school at Stanford University, and soon settled in San Francisco. Over the years, she has pursued numerous interests, including periods of practicing law, becoming a potter, working as a foundation program officer, studying art, and serving on nonprofit boards and councils. She has two wonderful daughters and two delightful grandchildren.

In the early 1970s, she collaborated with her father, John W. Gardner, on a collection of quotations, *Know or Listen to Those Who Know* (still in print as *Quotations of Wit and Wisdom*). Ten years ago, when her parents moved West, she and her father began work on a book of selected quotations from his fifty years of writing and speaking. This led to the present volume.

PART ONE

A Life
in Action—
and Reflection

Glimpses of My Life

John W. Gardner rarely wrote about his personal life. His subject was larger than himself; he focused on how to live truly and well, on strengthening society, on the America he loved, on the work to be done. Here we gather glimpses of the more private side of his life from his journals, speeches, essays, and books. "When the cage of memory opens," he said, "who knows what will fly out—something endearing or something heart-rending, a bird that will sing to us or one that will fix its talons in us?"

I was born in Los Angeles, California. When I was about a year old my mother decided to move out into the country eleven miles west of the city. There, in an area of lima bean fields as far as the eye could see, one of the first of the legendary California real estate developers had laid out a pattern of streets and had built the Beverly Hills Hotel nestled against the foothills.

We moved into the hotel, and my mother bought the nineteenth house in the development. It grew rapidly and soon had its own school, but there were still only three or four stores and one policeman, Charlie Blair. It was a very small country town. Everyone knew everyone else. It was a great place to grow up. There was no way for small boys to get into any serious trouble.

But it wasn't quite your typical American small town. Douglas Fairbanks and Mary Pickford were building a large place in the foothills. Movie stars were glimpsed from time to time. And the film companies shot some of their scenes on the streets of that peaceful place.

As a boy in California I spent a good deal of time in the Mother Lode country, and like every boy of my age I listened raptly to the tales told by the old-time prospectors in that area, some of them veterans of the Klondike gold rush. Every one of them had at least one good campfire story of a lost gold mine. The details varied: the original discoverer had died in the mine, or had gone crazy, or had been killed in a shooting scrape, or had just walked off thinking the mine worthless. But the central theme was constant: riches left untapped. I have come to believe that those tales offer a paradigm of education as most of us experience it. The mine is worked for a little while and then abandoned.

I attended Punahou School in Honolulu just after World War I, when I was seven years old and living with my grandparents. The school had a Christmas play. I was one of the Three Wise Men: a seven-year-old wise man in a Japanese kimono with a bath towel as a turban.

When the Three Wise Men marched on stage I was astonished and captivated by the sight of the audience. It seemed like thousands and thousands of people, though it could not have been more than three hundred. My grandparents were out there somewhere, and my friends, and their parents, and my teachers—and I had to locate them. It interfered somewhat with the modest duties of a wise man.

When the time came for the Three Wise Men to exit, two of them did so and the third remained studying the audience in utter fascination—until I heard my teacher's voice whispering urgently "Johnny, it's time to go!" I scampered off stage, the audience roared with laughter and I was deeply embarrassed.

So much for early promise.

━━━━━━━━

In the 1930s, college days were magical. Those were the days before students carried their test scores around as a blessed or ominous verdict, before the shadow of admission to graduate school hung like a Sword of Damocles. Modernity, that great bird of prey, had not yet fixed its talons in us.

I appreciate the enormous value of a liberal education. I've had my share of learning in the thick of life, but the college years were unique. I grew in every dimension—not just intellectually but in every other way. I sorted myself out. I enjoyed. I made dumb mistakes. I laid the basis of breadth and depth of interest that has given a greater richness to everything I've learned since.

It is not easy to tell young people how unpurposefully we learn, how life tosses us head over heels into our most vivid learning experiences, how intensely we resist many of the increments in our own growth. In my first two years at Stanford I had little time for studies. I was setting records in swimming, and dating required serious attention. But I did have one little burst of scholarly imagination, sparked by a $100 prize that the Colonial Dames were offering for the best essay on American History by an undergraduate. This was the Great Depression and I needed the money. So I wrote a piece on the New England fisheries. Somebody else won the prize, which did not surprise me.

The next day in my class in American History, Professor Thomas Bailey (a nationally known scholar) said, "I would like to see John Gardner in my office after class." Had I done something wrong?

When I arrived at his office, he was sitting at his desk wearing a green eyeshade. He said, "You know, you came within a hair of winning that Colonial Dames' prize. The only reason you didn't is that it was perfectly clear you hadn't been trained in research, and you did have a little tendency to exaggerate the role of the codfish in the American Revolution. But the judges were very impressed."

"Now," he said, "why are you getting a D in my course?"

I said, "Well, I love the lectures, but I am awfully busy on other things." I didn't elaborate on the "other things." I came away with the conviction that I had better take my studies more seriously, which no doubt was Professor Bailey's intention.

I was married in my senior year to a girl of extraordinary grace and beauty, Aida Marroquin. When we first met, two years earlier, she spoke no English and I could not converse in Spanish, but it was a negligible barrier.

It was unheard of in those days for an undergraduate to marry. One of my closest friends took me to the Peninsula Creamery for a milkshake and set out to persuade me that I was indulging an emotional impulse that would wreck my career. I listened patiently, but I wasn't convinced.

Any man who has been married to the same woman for many years has a special understanding of continuity. But the continuities are not incompatible with change or the need for change. In real life, the fact that people and institutions keep the same name over the years gives an illusion of stability that isn't there. I say that I've been married to the same woman for sixty-six years. In fact, it's the same name and the same social security number, but the person doesn't remain the same. Thanks to her capacity to grow and change, I've been married to a whole series of women over that period—each more delightful than her predecessor, I hasten to add.

When Aida and I were planning to marry, my mother offered me a plot of ground that was right next to two little student rentals that she owned. She said, "I will give you the ground if you build a house and look after the two rentals." I was a better mobilizer, even in those days, than I was a carpenter, so I got my brother, my two cousins, my stepfather and his two brothers, and we all built the house. My mother designed it.

It was the depth of the Great Depression, which turned out to be an excellent time to build. The owner of the lumberyard would meet me at the gate, he was so eager for customers. In 1934, everything was dirt cheap. We built the house for $1,600. There were essentially no labor costs, except for the plumbing and electrical work.

I remember the plumbing because the man who did it said something I've never forgotten. He came from some distance to take the job. One day he said, "Mr. Gardner, I have to leave early. I hate to leave a job early, but President Roosevelt is having one of his Fireside Chats tonight. I just feel that if he's willing to sit down and talk to us, I should be there to hear him."

Clearly he felt an almost personal bond with the President, and I counted it a remarkable testimony to leadership. It may also be testimony to the fact that radio was in some curious way a more intimate form of communication than television turned out to be.

The Bancroft Library at the University of California at Berkeley contained, among other things, one of the great collections on Spanish colonial days in the West, presided over by Herbert Bolton. I was working toward a Ph.D. in psychology, and Bolton's older brother Thaddeus was one of the distinguished figures in the early days of American psychology. Capitalizing on that thin connection, I paid a call on Bolton one day to obtain some guidance in the study of California history, a field I had no business paying attention to at that moment in my career. He worked on a reading list for me and I began a leisurely exploration of California history that has continued to this day.

It was, perhaps, an odd diversion for a psychologist, but it was just another theme in the omnivorous reading that began when I was five and continued for some forty years.

One day during World War II there occurred a wholly unexpected turning point in my thinking about life and the world. I was a Marine Corps officer stationed in Italy, thirty-two years old. There was a saying in the wartime military that life was "Hurry up and wait." At times you had to act in a desperate hurry, and other times you just had to wait. In one of the moments of waiting I was walking along a hillside when it occurred to me that my life had been turned upside down twice by events in the outside world—the Great Depression and World War II—yet I had never studied the economic, political, and social forces that produced such events. As a psychologist I had confined myself to individual behavior, leaving it to others to worry about the big world.

I concluded that I hadn't been very smart in that neglect, and wrote home for a couple of books, beginning a course of study that broadened and deepened over the years. In a sense, that day laid out the agenda for the rest of my life.

It took a good many years to come to the realization that teaching was in a sense my life work. I began teaching when I was twenty-three and I wasn't very good at it. Nor did I like it very much. When I left Mount Holyoke after Pearl Harbor, I was pretty sure I wouldn't be teaching in the future.

When I first arrived in Washington in 1942, I was asked to head the Latin American section of the Foreign Broadcast Intelligence Service. Since I had a good knowledge of the Spanish language and of Latin America, I had no doubt of my intellectual capacity to handle the job. I was astounded when I began to receive good marks on my management skills. It was wholly contrary to my image of myself, wholly at odds with my plans for the future. I was twenty-nine years old and had never run anything. I had no ambition to run anything. From my earliest years, I had thought of myself as a student, an observer, pleasantly detached from the mainstream of the world's action. From that point on, my life was to be governed by constant conflict between the life of action and the life of reflection.

In later years when I found myself in leadership roles, I discovered that teaching was an absolutely necessary part of leading. In the only kind of leadership our society can really admire, leaders explain. They communicate the facts and reasons that people need to know if they are to reach wise decisions. They teach by precept and example, in speeches, in writing, in exemplary acts.

I found that I liked teaching, and when my active leadership days were winding down, I returned to the classroom. In my course on leadership at Stanford University, I pointed out that the best leaders are incessantly teaching, and the best teachers are leading.

———————

The year my mother passed the hundred-year mark, she called me and said, "You know this business of aging bothers me so, I can hardly stand it. I find it terribly upsetting."

I said, "But think how lucky you are that you're physically healthy and mentally alert."

"Oh, I'm not talking about myself," She said. "I'm talking about you and your brother."

And more recently, I had news of a ninety-nine-year-old friend in the East. I was told that he had occasional lucid intervals, which pleased me enormously. I must say, without wanting to brag, that I've been having lucid intervals all my life—and they have not diminished in frequency since I turned eighty. That's why the news of my ninety-nine-year-old friend was so thrilling. I could name people half his age—some of them in high places—who would be lucky to have occasional lucid intervals.

━━━━━━━━━

I don't think of myself in lofty terms. Looking back over the years I see a California boy finding his way through life, endlessly challenged, surmounting obstacles, falling on his face, regretting that he hadn't done better, always studying, always trying, always wondering. . . .

2

In the President's Cabinet

From 1965 to 1968, John W. Gardner was Secretary of Health, Education, and Welfare. Those were the years in which the Great Society programs were put in place. He was involved in the launching of Medicare, carried out the first enforcement of the Civil Rights Act, and presided over the sweeping programs mandated by twenty-eight pieces of landmark legislation, such as the Elementary and Secondary Education Act, the Air Quality Act of 1967, and the law creating the Corporation for Public Broadcasting. It was a time of turmoil in the cities over issues of race and poverty and of growing civil unrest over the escalating Vietnam War. Ever the optimist, he commented early in his tenure, "What we have before us are breathtaking opportunities disguised as insoluble problems."

Many years later, in the 1990s, Gardner talked about the HEW years as he told stories of his life on tape. Because he was reluctant to spend time looking backward when he saw so much work to be done for the future, he did not review or edit the resulting text. What follows is a small portion of the material, carefully edited to preserve voice and meanings.

When I was Secretary of Health, Education, and Welfare I was a bit in awe of the history of Washington. Every day on the way to work I'd see the monuments—the Washington Monument, the Lincoln Memorial, the Jefferson Memorial and the Capitol. It was an awesome spectacle.

Any tourist will tell you that. I'd think of the men who founded the country and the people who kept this country going and hope I was equal to the challenges before me. To know you're a part of that history, and you're expected to live up to it, is humbling.

THE THEATER OF HIGH OFFICE

I knew the position of Secretary of Health, Education, and Welfare was a big job, but was not prepared for the extraordinary infrastructure, the enormously diverse support that a top executive has in that position. I had been the head of the Carnegie Corporation in New York with a staff of thirty-six. I was now head of the Department of Health, Education, and Welfare with a staff of 105,000, and all that went with it. It was the "all that went with it" that I was not prepared for. I had eight people just to handle my correspondence. They were not letter writers, they were people who made sure that if somebody lower down could answer a letter, the Social Security commissioner for example, it went to him. They routed the letters and made sure there were replies. We literally had about a thousand letters a week sent over from the White House, letters that had been addressed to the President but were properly answered by my department. The eight-person correspondence team was a busy little group.

I had a legislative assistant secretary. I had a security officer. I had two speech writers. Practically every phase of my job was covered by somebody, and in many cases, people who were superbly qualified to do the job. I had a limousine, of course, with a wonderful driver who was my constant companion for years, and a very fine companion he was. There was a telephone in my car. I thought, "How convenient for me!"—until I realized that the real point of the telephone was to make sure the President could reach me. I have to laugh, in retrospect. What I thought of as convenience was anything but. As a member of the President's cabinet, you're never out of touch, you are more locked into the job than most people ever can imagine.

I had a lot more support available to me than I ever used. For example, I was allowed to put in for one of the fleet of Lockheed jets the President had for sending people around the country. When I learned about this, I thought I'd use it. I was going to Hot Springs, Arkansas, and air connections were not easy. It was the way to travel. No waiting in lines. Just go to the plane. They took me to my destination and they waited for me. When the speech was over, I walked out, got in the plane, and returned to Washington. The next week I made the mistake of asking my comptroller how much that cost. I never used the planes again.

THE POLITICAL JUNGLE

When I went down to Washington, a friend said, "John, don't take the job. Washington will eat you alive, it's an absolute jungle. The country will lose a good educational leader, and it won't gain a good politician." He was right about its being a jungle, a lot of little men with blowguns and poison arrows, but he was wrong to think they would eat me for breakfast. I did not have any trouble surviving.

I didn't know a thing about Congress, but I knew the agencies and had many friends. They almost uniformly told me that the Department of Health, Education, and Welfare was a mess. Some said it was unmanageable, some said it was hopeless, a bunch of warring tribes. I had the very pleasant experience of discovering they were wrong. In fact, HEW was not well organized, it wasn't coordinated, it was just a group of agencies. But there were very good people in it at every level.

I want the Department of Health, Education, and Welfare to live in an environment of ideas. I want discussion of where the Department is headed and why, and what that means for government policy and for the future of the Nation. I want argument about what the most important problems are, and whether we're turning our backs on them or solving them or making them worse. I want criticism of our basic assumptions.

—The Secretary's Letter, Department of Health,
Education and Welfare, July 1967

I had strong people whom I came to rely on for a lot of the managing, but they just couldn't do many of the leadership tasks. They weren't visible enough and they didn't have the attention of the media the way a cabinet member did. HEW had a terrible image because nobody told the story of the department. It became clear that my job as the leader was to tell the story. The story I told was: "Our goal is to proctor human fulfillment within a framework of values and laws. We deal with obstacles to human fulfillment, whether poverty, or ignorance, or sickness, or trouble with the police. We're the department of people." I don't know if I convinced anybody in the great American public, but the people in the department loved it. Nobody had ever said what they were about as a department. When I started there were fourteen agencies. Nobody had ever said why they belonged together.

I had a job of leadership to do with our constituencies out there, with the Congress, with the media, and more. But the job also involved basic management. How do you manage fourteen agencies? The first thing was to get them down to eleven agencies. Beyond that, there were three key tools. One was the budget, the tool that allows you to really get a hold on the things. Another, of considerable interest to me, was personnel. This was maybe the most important thing. I dropped everything when a high post had to be filled. I had to have the right person in that job. I could not just say, "You folks go find him." I wanted to have a hand in it. And I did. Legislation was the third control. I wanted to know what legislative proposals were going out. I looked at them with great care and I gave my input if I had any problem with them.

Some of the top people at HEW could have run a corporation or succeeded at almost anything. They were good people, but, curiously, I was almost uniformly warned against them. I attribute this to a tendency to think that strong people are trouble. The Budget Bureau said, "Look out for so-and-so." The White House said, "Look out for so-and-so." And invariably the "so-and-sos" were the strong ones. It took very little time to realize they were my best allies. And they remained my best allies. They were the people I didn't have to clean up after. When they did something, they did it right. They would sometimes be a problem to deal with when purposes

Living, Leading, and the American Dream

crossed, because they were used to getting their way, or they were skilled at getting their way. But I found that, on the whole, I could work with them and they were tremendous allies.

One of the top people was obviously somewhat hostile to me when I first arrived, ready to take me on. He was strong, entrenched, and sure of his power. I soon realized that he was a very valuable person if I could get him on my side. The first breakthrough occurred when an issue came up that was very difficult to get over, to succeed in, to get the department to accept. He was in a position to glue it in, just from the virtue of his position and the respect he had. By the same token, he was maybe the only one who could put it across. I went to him and said, "L., I've got a real tough problem here. I think there's just one person in this department who can make it go and that's you." He signed on and we were allies from that time forward.

I'd rather work with strong people and take the occasional heat of conflict than work with weak people and have to mop up after them. There is an old saying that there's a kind of executive who separates the men from the boys and then hires the boys. He doesn't want strength around him. To me, nothing could be more self-destructive in an organization.

THE LEADER AS SYMBOL

Anyone heading a large organization needs to appreciate the symbolic nature of the office. There is a great deal of theater in high public office. You never walk into a room alone, you always have aides flanking you. It took me awhile to recognize the extent to which I was a symbol. One day, I went to visit the mailroom, a busy place, full of hardworking people. I just wanted to get a look at it. I spent about ten or fifteen minutes there, asking people about their jobs. The story of my visit went like wildfire around the department within a matter of days. I wasn't just a curious human being, I was a symbol of the folks up there, none of whom had ever been in the mailroom before.

Another day, my assistant came in and said, "There is a group of neuropsychiatrists meeting here in the department. They'd love to have you come in and say a few words to them." I said, "Bob, what in the heck would I have to say to neuropsychiatrists at 9:30 on a Monday morning?" Very calmly, he said, "Well, it would mean so much if you would just come in and talk to them for ten minutes." He rarely pressed me unless he really thought I ought to do something, but I just couldn't stomach the idea of talking off the top of my head to a group I wasn't prepared for. On the way down, I thought, "I'll ask them questions."

When I got there, about fifteen to twenty people were in the room. I said, "You folks have been meeting for a day and a half. What are the main problems that bother you? What causes you the most concern?" As we talked, I began to understand that it wasn't a message from me they wanted. They wanted to see the guy who, at the stroke of a pen, might affect their profession. To them, this was just a great big faceless bureaucracy, and the guy with the most influence was a stranger. They had heard of him, but they had never met him.

This was one of many indications, thousands over the years, that we want to take each other's measure face-to-face. We're more primitive than we think. The memo doesn't do it. We want to hear the tone of voice and see the body language. It gave me a whole new sense of things I had to do because of my position. What mattered was not just what I thought or what I was ready to talk about, but my role as a representative, a human representative in a big, anonymous government. It was a good lesson.

I had the feeling that I was a long way from the grass roots. This concerned me. I'd written *Self-Renewal,* in which I emphasized the importance of the front line experiences that lead to renewal. As you go up the line, you're more and more fed with statistics, indices, charts, graphs, symbolic communication. You don't know the soldier on the front line or the salesman behind the counter or the nurse looking after a patient. You don't know what they're experiencing, what they're thinking about, what a piece of legislation means to them. I never came close to solving that problem of breaking through the distance at HEW. I would plan to visit a laboratory, a storefront clinic, or some other site. The word that the Secretary was com-

Living, Leading, and the American Dream

ing would go out like lightning. By the time I arrived, everything was swept up, cleaned up, painted, and everybody was standing at the front door. It was not a casual inspection. Nevertheless, dealing with my people in various cities and through my other contacts, I got moderately close to the people who worked for the department.

The lesson of my first months was that I had big, powerful constituencies out there: the whole medical profession, the nurses, the psychiatrists, the pharmaceutical world, the whole teaching profession, the whole world of higher education, the world of science. They were basically friendly. They wanted to think well of the Secretary of HEW. They wanted to hear from me, and they wanted to take my measure.

I set out, quite proactively, to establish contacts with these constituencies. If I was invited to speak at the annual meeting of the dentists, I did it. I would go out of my way to be available because external relations were a big piece of my job. There were basically three parts to this: Congress, the media, and the constituencies in health, education, and welfare. (The White House was important but it was anything but external.) I had a hard time at the beginning because I was determined to make every speech count and to make it just right for the occasion. I was reducing the number of engagements because I couldn't accept what my speechwriters did for me. They were good, but I was used to writing my own speeches.

One day, I was sitting next to a nun at the head table at a luncheon in San Francisco. She said, "You must give a lot of speeches."

"Yes," I said, "but I don't give as many as I would like to because it's so hard to write them."

"Why don't you give the same speech every time, so you don't have to write so much?"

"Well, that doesn't seem right, to just give the same speech over and over."

She looked at me as though I were feebleminded and turned in her seat to face me. "Mr. Secretary, if it's the truth, why wouldn't you want to say it every single day?" The message got through.

BUREAUCRACY

One of the first problems I encountered was what I called fire fighting. People were running from this place to that. Everything seemed a crisis. Everything seemed to have to be settled by sundown. I tried to get people to plan ahead and discovered, somewhat to my amusement, that there are people who just love the fire fighting. They love that sense of, "Gee, I've got to do this and I've got to do that and I've got to get them both done by sundown." I said to my staff, "Look, let's get the longest planning phase that we can on everything we do. Cut down the number of things that seem urgent, focus only on the crisis where you really have to get it done by sundown. Don't just run around." The problem with fire fighting is that it is contagious. Soon, everybody is running around like chickens with their heads cut off.

In Washington the person who rushes to put out every minor blaze is "someone who gets things done." If he pauses to think about next week's fire, he's "an impractical visionary." If he strikes a pose as he pours water on last week's dead ashes, he's a statesman.

—Journals

I came to admire bureaucrats. They had their problems. They were extremely skilled in the arts of self-defense and extremely skilled at the low profile. Often, you would hardly know they were involved in something—you had to smoke out who had made this decision or that. But many of them were good—and devoted. They really wanted to do a good job. They believed in what they were doing. Yet, within any four-year period, they didn't know what the political philosophy was going to be or whether doctrines they'd been living by were going to be turned upside down. It's not surprising that they learned to keep a low profile and ride out trouble. Lyndon Johnson once said, "There are times when you just have to hunker down like a jackass in a snowstorm." They were good at it. They were good at getting as much of what they valued as they could in whatever regime

Living, Leading, and the American Dream

they were in. The ones who were fairly prominent had to keep their lines out to the media and their lines out to Congress. Some of them had their own lines into the White House and into the professional constituencies. They were pretty gifted people.

Many skilled bureaucrats had a lot of political know-how. There was a Congressman, a nice, polite man, who proceeded so cautiously that he never left a footprint. He was a swing vote and I needed his vote on one matter on which he had not expressed support. I dug around but people just didn't know where he stood. I talked with some of my folks. They said, "Well, he has had some dealings with NIH, why don't you talk to Jim Shannon." Jim, the head of the National Institutes of Health, was a very good politician who never seemed so. His persona was that of a research administrator. I called him up and gave him the name of this Congressman. He said, "do you know so-and-so," naming a very powerful industrialist. I did. "Call him up and state your case. You may want to say that you need this man's vote or maybe you don't want to say it, but state your case." I made the call and got the Congressman's vote almost immediately. Jim Shannon was a gifted bureaucrat who knew how to handle the situation.

CONGRESS

When I first took the job as Secretary of Health, Education, and Welfare, I was very familiar with government agencies. I'd worked for perhaps seven of them as a consultant, I knew the ins and outs, the rhythm of the work. I knew very little about Congress. I had testified in perhaps two hearings. So I started to talk to members of Congress. I talked to perhaps six different Congressmen whom I knew and trusted to talk straight to me. I think the best was Senator Jacob Javits of New York. He said, "Remember one word, *consult.* These folks don't like surprises. You do not need to get yourself in the position of having to take their advice, you can always tell them you're consulting a number of people, but they want to be in the loop. They don't want to go to lunch in the Senate lunch room and learn about something you're doing that bears on their committee and they didn't know about it."

Others told me that just below the surface of every Congressman's consciousness is a deep suspicion of the executive branch, a fear that the bureaucrats will out-maneuver them, cover up, evade, and get their way. I learned that there is a certain paranoia in members of Congress which, at its most normal and healthy, isn't really paranoia at all because people *are* out to get them. They know they have people who want their job. That's part of the game.

I took enormous pains, once I began to understand the system, to not exacerbate that suspicion and paranoia. As Secretary of HEW, I was presiding over a warehouse full of goodies, so to speak, for congressional districts. And naturally, people in Congress would make requests to benefit their district—either to ease up on a regulatory prosecution or investigation, or to grant them a water pollution laboratory or food and drug installation of some kind. Obviously I had to turn down most such requests. These decisions came through due process, through investigation and judgment by the division heads involved. If I had to turn down a Congressman two or three times, I would find an occasion to stop by his office within the next several weeks just to say hello, maybe to ask some advice. They always seemed to value that.

I noted previously that I liked to work with strong people. With Congress, this was particularly true. You might have a tough time convincing some prickly or difficult members, but they could deliver results if you succeeded. John Fogerty, chairman of the Subcommittee on Appropriations for HEW, was a guy who made it clear in the first interview that he'd seen Secretaries come and go. They didn't impress him. But John, if you convinced him, carried your groceries right through his subcommittee onto the floor and through the floor. It was wrapped up if Fogerty believed you.

On the other hand, there was a wonderful fellow named Carl Perkins. He was just the nicest man to deal with. He was sweet, he was very gentle. He was friendly and he wanted friendly relations. But he didn't carry the battle for you. You could convince him and still not get anywhere because he wasn't going to get into a fight.

I ended up liking politicians. They were often not likable on the surface, but I was very conscious of the kind of life they led and the forces that were impinging on them. I was absolutely at odds with Senators Sam Ervin and Richard Russell on civil rights, obviously, and I would have some rather stiff sessions with them and other Southerners in Congress. But there was a courtesy in the way they dealt with me that I found very compatible. It permitted us to be in flat out conflict and still find it a tolerable situation. I remember Richard Russell saying to me, when I sat down in his office to talk about civil rights, "Well, you understand, Mr. Secretary, that I'm just dead against what you're doing. I'm just absolutely in opposition to what you're doing. I think that it's bad for my state, bad for the South, and it isn't good public policy." He said it very politely and in a very civil way, but clearly he was laying it right on the line. I responded, "Well, I understand that, I understand what's going on. I realize that we are, in fact, coercing many of your people to follow a path which they've not traditionally followed. But I have to remind you that I'm doing it to enforce the law that came out of this institution. The Senate and the House passed this law, I'm enforcing it, and as long as I'm Secretary, I will continue to enforce it." We went on then to various details. There was something orderly and civil to be respected about each side stating their case clearly.

One case was a no-win situation. It involved John Pastori, a very good friend of the department. We were in the middle of a fight to get some legislation passed. He was our champion; he was eloquent, fiery and resourceful. We valued him enormously. One day, he came to us and said that he wanted us to withdraw a regulation we had recently issued, which he found was totally unacceptable. He said that if we didn't, he was not going to help on the legislation which he'd been championing on our behalf. We were in a quandary. If we withdrew the regulation, we would have withdrawn something we had thought very hard about. If we went ahead with it, we'd lose Pastori's loyal efforts on our behalf.

After serious consideration, we decided to withdraw the regulation. That seemed to me the end of the fight. But Wilbur Cohen, an undersecretary who was a very experienced government person, said, "We should withdraw the regulation, and then revise it." Which we did. We went over every single word that bothered Pastori. We asked ourselves if there were ways of saying the same thing that would not bother him or would bother him less. Our rewritten regulation was accepted by Pastori. It wasn't that different, but we had taken it out of the arena of anger, conflict and test of wills.

Wilbur Cohen taught me a lot of lessons. This was just one of them. In a conflict where I'm standing for one position and ready to fall on my sword if I don't get it, and somebody else is in complete opposition, there are probably seven intermediate positions that you can repair to that take the heat out of it. A word change, a phrasing change, and you find a ground for moving ahead. I've used that successfully many times.

In the examples I've given, I was dealing with strong-minded but reasonable people. In all phases of high office where combat is involved, you have to recognize that occasionally you run into someone whose paranoia has reached a point where he's very hard to deal with. Such people don't last, as a rule. They take things personally, they take defeat personally, they take conflict personally. This is almost always an ailment of the politician who has battle fatigue and is moving into bitterness, paranoia and self-pity.

I came away feeling it was terribly important to understand how Congress worked: to respect the difficulty of the job, to respect the best people there, to respect the good parts of those who weren't the best, and to understand the system even if it was your intention to fight it. After my years as a lobbyist (after all, I spent twelve years lobbying as Secretary of HEW, and as head of Common Cause, and the Urban Coalition), I concluded that the Congress was the accessible branch. You could get to a Congressman much more easily than to a middle-level bureaucrat in HEW (or any large agency) who did you in or who made the decision that made trouble for your industry or your institution. I came to respect some of the power brokers, the very powerful Senators, who really moved the system, even if we didn't agree a great deal of the time.

Russell Long, the very powerful chairman of the Finance Committee, was an excellent example. He and I disagreed on a lot of subjects, and he had gotten a lot of taxpayers' money funneled into Louisiana for interests that were dear to him. Then I saw a tax bill in so much trouble that it seemed hopeless. Everybody was hanging a different ornament on the tree, getting their little tax break, their little tax loophole. It just stalled. There were many conflicting interests and bitterness was developing.

Russell Long went to work, calling in his chits and putting the arm on people who were preventing a solution from being reached. Pretty soon he had a tax bill and Congress had a vote on it. He respected the system. He knew the system and understood how to make it work. I came to see the value of that, especially when I watched young idealists lose over and over again on issues important to me. They lost because they never bothered to understand how the system worked. They essentially didn't really respect the system.

THE ADMINISTRATION

I had very good relations with President Johnson. It was a relationship of mutual trust and respect, and on the whole, a very satisfying team relationship. But in the federal government, your personal relationships go just so far, and then you're dealing with institutions. As any former cabinet or sub-cabinet member or division chief will tell you, you're dealing with the White House, not just the President. It can be an obstacle and a frustration because it's inevitably bureaucracy. But it can also be an opportunity. I counted it as an opportunity to deal with multiple individuals rather than just the President. The thing you have to remember about the President is the tyranny of the clock. There just isn't time for him to do everything himself.

Joe Califano told me that when he was Secretary of Health, Education, and Welfare, he required all of his people to go through him to the White House so that he could control the communications. I would have found this very limiting. I had as many as eight or ten people who could go in and out of the White House on good terms. They would establish their own ties with White House subordinates, the people below the Vice President and the President's staff. What that meant for me was a certain lack of control.

If I had eight or ten people out there, I couldn't know whether they were all giving the precise message I would have wanted them to give. The upside and advantage was that I had eight or ten channels to get messages in and to get word out of the White House: the gossip, the relationships, the state of affairs. I found it more than worth the occasional disorder of multiple access.

Relations with the other people within the administration (cabinet relationships, relationships with subcabinet agencies) were very important and also touchy. There is a kind of courtesy between cabinet members, but also subsurface resistance. Even if a cabinet member agrees, his agency heads may not agree and *they* may sabotage you.

Getting the whole administration to pull together was critically important with civil rights. I had to put in place the first enforcement of the civil rights legislation. The more I studied it, the more apparent it became that we had to be utterly consistent. What we were doing was forcing a fairly deep change in a culture by coercion, by legislation. We were saying, "There's a piece of your culture that you've got to root out." This was serious business. Even someone who believed as deeply as I did in the cause had to recognize that this was tough stuff. The least you could do was be absolutely clear and consistent as to what you wanted.

There remained inconsistencies within the administration itself. If I got the slightest wind of it, I'd jump in my car, go and see the person involved, and say, "You know, it's very tough to administer this, we've just got to hold the line." It worked.

Unfortunately, this approach broke down when Nixon became President. It wasn't that Nixon himself had done something. The Secretary of HEW would say one thing, somebody in the Department of Justice would say something different. The loss of unity began to undermine the whole thing so that people could say, "We don't know what the law is."

One of the most satisfying things about working with President Johnson was his intimate knowledge of the workings of government and particularly, of course, the workings of Congress. He could advise you on almost any incident that was occurring because he knew the people, he knew the rules of the game, he knew all the intricacies. He was rather scornful of some of the people full of good intentions who didn't always keep track of all the details. Once he asked Hubert Humphrey if he had checked a certain swing vote on a committee vote, a vote they weren't sure of. Humphrey said, "Yes, he's going to vote for us." Johnson asked Humphrey when he had talked to him. Humphrey replied, "I talked to him four days ago." Johnson said, "That's not good enough, I want to know what he's saying today." As soon as Humphrey left, Johnson picked up the phone, called Bobby Baker, his close aide, and said, "I want you to find out as of now how he's going to vote in that committee meeting *today.*"

One day, before my HEW term, I was talking with Johnson when he was Senate Majority Leader. Richard Russell came in. Russell, the Senator from Georgia, was probably the most respected Senator at the time and was very close to Johnson. He had a minute or two of exchange with Johnson, then started for the door. Johnson said, "Oh, by the way, Dick, how are you going to vote on that issue this afternoon in committee?" Russell threw his arms up in a kind of expansive gesture and said, "Lyndon, you know I'm your friend." Johnson replied, "That's not what I asked you." And this is the precision of congressional dealings. If you make a commitment, you make a commitment, and it's explicit and you're expected to keep it explicit.

Very few of the anecdotes about Lyndon Johnson are about this meticulous style, his close knowledge of detail, this really quite disciplined side of him. The journalists and the public enjoyed the character of the expansive, aggressive, colorful Texan. I remember one story that was very widely circulated at the time. He was at Andrews Air Force Base about to go to Camp David, and was chatting with a couple of his aides. There were a number of helicopters parked outside and a young lieutenant in the Air Force came up and sought the President's attention and when he got it, he said, "Mr. President, that helicopter parked right next to the door is yours." And Johnson was said to have replied, "Son, all of those helicopters are mine." I wonder about the accuracy of such stories. I saw another side of the President, and I must say it helped me do my job.

DEPARTURE FROM THE CABINET

It was November of 1967 when President Johnson told his cabinet that he was planning one or more cabinet dinners at which they could share ideas concerning the presidential campaign of 1968. How might we make the strongest case for the reelection of Johnson?

As I thought over the major accomplishments of 1965–1967, I believed that a strong case could in fact be made. Shortly after the first dinner I wrote a memo to Joseph Califano laying it out, building primarily on the segment of the administration I knew best. Focusing my mind on what should happen next had a truly disruptive consequence. It dawned on me—slowly but powerfully—that I did not believe Lyndon Johnson should run for reelection. It was not a half-formed thought—it was a solid conviction. During the second dinner, I was virtually silent. I knew then that I had to resign my post.

Before I did so, I produced a summary of the department's achievements during my tenure. Then, in early January, I wrote a very brief letter of resignation and delivered it by hand to the President. He read it and asked me why. I said that in my judgment the course of events had so damaged his capacity to lead that he could not unite the country in the struggles that lay ahead. I did not know that within three months Martin Luther King Jr. would be assassinated, and two months later Senator Robert Kennedy would meet the same fate. But I was intimately familiar with the urban riots and the campus disorders and I knew that the nation needed—desperately—a steadying hand. I was certain that President Johnson could not provide that steadying hand.

I explained this to the President as best I could. It wasn't easy. I gave him great credit for what he had achieved in my department, but I kept returning to my point. I said that in an election year, a President contemplating reelection deserved the wholehearted backing of his entire team, and that I could not give it.

He spent a half-hour cross-examining me to find out if I had some grievance he could deal with. I stuck to my one point. There were other matters on which we might have debated our differences, but I didn't want anything to detract from my main message.

Finally, he sighed and said he and Lady Bird had discussed very seriously whether he should withdraw. He then uttered sentences he would use in much the same form as when he finally announced his withdrawal. It was not a new thought to him; he was not fumbling for words.

What did it do to our relationship? I think it strengthened it. Having told him forthrightly just about the hardest thing one could say to a President, I think he trusted me more. We remained on terms of friendship and mutual respect to the end of his life.

Some people seem to believe that for each public problem there is a solution readily available—a solution that can be promptly achieved by passing a law and voting some money.

It is the vending-machine concept of social change. Put a coin in the machine and out comes a piece of candy. If there is a social problem, pass a law and out comes a solution. When the nation fails to solve one of its problems promptly, people who hold such a simplified view naturally assume that someone in power was stupid or misguided or both.

I don't want to rule that out as a possibility. But the truth is that we face a number of extremely puzzling problems to which no one has the answers.

—*No Easy Victories*, 1968, p. 28

Let me close with just a word or two about my experience with the great department of Health, Education, and Welfare, which no longer exists. I thoroughly enjoyed the action. I found the role of a public figure reasonably rewarding. There was a lot that stimulated me, led me to grow, led me to learn. On the other hand, all my life, I've moved back and forth between action and reflection, and this was a period of undiluted action. I missed the downtime for reflection, for reading, for sorting out my thoughts. At HEW, it was action, action all the way.

I mentioned the theater of high public office. There is almost a requirement that you be something of an actor, something of a ham, something of an exhibitionist, which was very contrary to my nature. I'm happy to say I acquired a fair amount of skill in this department. I learned how to bring an audience to its feet. I learned to get my point across in ways that weren't prosaic and flat. For me, being Secretary of HEW was an enormous period of growth, an enormous challenge. I found it extremely rewarding to understand how our government worked and how the nation functioned. I saw America from a vantage point I could never have seen it from had it not been for that position.

3

Leading Common Cause

On August 18, 1970, John W. Gardner announced the formation of Common Cause, a citizens' movement with the ambitious goal of holding government accountable. The nation's capital abounds in wise and weary observers who know all the reasons why any new venture is bound to fail—and they saw little hope for it. But by the end of the first year it had more than two hundred thousand members.

In the years that followed, Common Cause and its members played a leading role in bringing about greater openness and accountability in our national government. They promoted (and won) legislation for a new way of financing presidential election campaigns, successfully pressured Congress to legislate an end to the Vietnam War, and facilitated the greatest wave of state government reform in our nation's history.

The focus was on process, on repairing the system. In an interview, Gardner once said: "I think of people sitting in an ancient automobile by the side of the road. The tires are flat and the drive shaft is bent, but they're engaged in a great argument as to whether they should go to Phoenix or San Francisco. In my imagination, I am standing by the road saying, "You're not going anywhere till you fix the darn car.""

When we founded Common Cause I believed we were enlisting in a war that would never end. The impulses to lie, cheat, steal and defraud will never die. The swindlers and charlatans and well-dressed crooks who prey on the citizen by manipulating the political process will always be with us. It was our intention to mount a counter force that would speak for citizens and we have done so.

The movement didn't get off the ground to the sound of universal applause. Just for the fun of it, I dipped back into the records of our early days. The critics from the right cut us up for being radical, the critics from the left damned us as elitist and conservative. I was described in most unflattering terms, terms I wouldn't care to repeat. I still have every clipping. I stick pins in them.

But the early mail more than made up for it. Here are some quotes:

One read: "God bless you. . . . You will save the Republic."

Another: "Thanks for doing what you're doing . . . I don't want to be patted on the head any more."

Another: "Dear Don Quixote: I always admire a man ready to attack windmills."

A letter in our second year said: "Last year I was poor and skeptical and sent $5. I'm still poor but less skeptical. Here's $15.

And then there was the letter from a young prison inmate: "I was very skeptical about Common Cause . . . I didn't think the Peace Corps would make it either. But then I didn't think I would ever be in San Quentin. It is evident that I haven't been thinking very clearly . . ."

We received plenty of compliments from the press. I have those clippings, too—laminated. When you find yourself wringing your hands over the sins of the media, try to remember that the rise of Common Cause was greatly helped by friendly attention from the press.

But without doubt, in those early days, the most dazzling compliments were the ones we gave ourselves. Self-affirmation is essential to morale, and I must say that, as Shakespeare put it, we laid it on with a trowel. We knew we were good, and we believed in full disclosure.

The first board meetings were tumultuous. Handling 60 eager citizen board members who were absolutely certain they were going to save the world was an experience.

GIVING THE NATION BACK TO THE PEOPLE

Common Cause, by linking the long tradition of citizen action with the skills of professional lobbying, introduced a new ingredient into the political system, a means of assuring continuous accountability to the citizen— a means of voting between elections. We think it's time to give this nation back to its people. We share the cheerful conviction that as citizens we have every right to raise hell when we see injustice done, or the public interest betrayed, or the public process corrupted. The basic ailments that are making invalids of our political and governmental institutions will only be cured by tough, sustained pressure. And that pressure must come from citizens.

Today good citizens leave the voting booth, pat themselves on the back for doing their civic duty, and then go home and forget the whole thing. But representatives of the special interests are in their offices the morning after election day figuring out the next step. Politics is the only game where the real action begins after the public has filed out the stadium.

We don't want to take the politics out of politics. We just want to take the rascals out of politics. We know we'll never wholly succeed. But we're going to make it a lot tougher for politicians to pursue rascality as a reputable way of life. We agree with the Chinese proverb, "You can't keep the birds of sorrow from flying over your head, but you can keep them from building nests in your hair."

INSTRUMENTS OF SELF-GOVERNMENT

There isn't any possibility that we can make power less seductive nor banish from politics all those who will abuse power once they get it. What we can do is to devise realistic arrangements that will make it more difficult to separate citizens from the levers of power, more difficult for a tightly knit inner circle to monopolize those levers.

Effectiveness, access, responsiveness, accountability—these are the attributes we have a right to expect of our instruments of self-government.

The problem is not power as such—in the presidency, in the private sector or anywhere else. The problem is power that is not held accountable. Too often our elected representatives feel accountable first and foremost to the donors who finance their campaigns. In other words we no longer have a government "deriving its just powers from the consent of the governed."

The problem in campaign financing was never more clearly expressed than by Congressman Eddie Garmatz, who was chairman of the Committee on Merchant Marine and Fisheries in the House. Reporters asked him if it wasn't improper for a committee chairman who had the power of decision over important maritime matters to get large campaign gifts from the maritime industry. He said, "Who in the hell do you expect me to get it from? The post office people? The bankers? You get it from the people who you helped some way or another. It's only natural." No wonder we've seen so many moral midgets in the seats of the mighty.

There must be a better way.

Common Cause has fought long and hard to achieve rational controls on campaign financing. To illustrate the extraordinary difficulties we have encountered, let me tell a truly demoralizing little story. As long ago as 1913 Congress began considering a limit on the size of individual campaign contributions. Finally, in 1940 the reform was enacted into law. For thirty-one years thereafter members of Congress lived happily with the new law, for the simple reason that no one seemed to mind if they violated the ceiling. No attorney general in all those thirty-one years ever tried to enforce it.

In 1971 Common Cause sued the major parties, seeking to restrain the politicians from breaking the law. The parties denied that we had standing to sue and moved to dismiss the suit. A federal judge rejected their motion. For the first time there was a possible alternative path of enforcement for the 1940 statute, namely, citizen action through the courts. *Congress promptly repealed the statute.* If there was danger of its being enforced, elected representatives wanted no part of it.

In short, a reform that was urged the year after I was born—and that's about as far back as you can go—was enacted twenty-eight years later, was an unenforced scandal for thirty-one more years, and then was cynically repealed when enforcement loomed as a possibility.

Everyone senses the corrupting power of money, but few grasp the power of secrecy to subvert the public process. I received my education back in the days when all schoolchildren had to study Latin—and I remember an ancient Latin saying on secrecy: *Amphora sub veste numquam portatur honeste.* It means "No one carries a jug under his coat for an honest reason." I have the feeling that the ancient Romans would have understood our politics.

Corruption, backroom fixes, secret deals—quite aside from their moral repulsiveness—finally create government that just doesn't work. Finally, the "insiders" can't even save themselves. The intricately rigged system fails to serve even those who rigged it.

—Speech to National Conference of Bar Presidents
and National Association of Bar Executives, Atlanta, 1976

PLAY TO WIN

The citizen advocacy group must be willing to play hardball. If the contest is a polite tennis match that you can win or lose with a genteel laugh, then it is not worth your time. Play by the rules but play to win. We must not become combatants in a noble cause who love the righteous posturing so much that victory becomes a secondary consideration. Every citizen group should hang on its wall the "Peanuts" cartoon that shows Charlie Brown on the pitching mound saying, "How can we lose when we're so sincere?"

In 1973, Common Cause played the key outside lobbying role in persuading the House of Representatives to reverse its long tradition of secrecy and open up most of its bill-drafting sessions. Soon after, Congressman Charles W. Dent was planning to hold a meeting of his subcommittee of the House Administration Committee. A member of Common Cause's Congressional Monitoring Project, a polite and dignified young woman named Connie Keneally, was in the room. She was told that it was a closed meeting. She pointed out courteously that under House rules, every meeting was open until the committee voted in open session to close it. She said that if such a vote were passed she would gladly leave the room. The chairman blew up. He gathered his committee and staff and stormed out of the room. She followed. They went into a congressman's private office and when she entered, she was put out.

Charles Dent is from Pennsylvania. The next day the leading newspaper in Pittsburgh carried a story headed "Congressman Dent Defies House Rules!" Several months later he was still trying to explain himself to anyone who would listen. But it's *hard* to explain. All he had to do to get our representative to leave the room was to follow the House rules and get his committee to vote the meeting closed. Why didn't he take that obvious course?

The answer is, he was very angry. I have now seen the reaction often enough to tell you why he was angry. He was angry because an individual who claimed no power, wealth, rank or title other than that of citizen of the United States dared to call him to account. A mere citizen was requiring him, with great politeness, to obey the rules he should have obeyed without prompting. One of the great strengths of Common Cause is that we don't believe there's any such thing as a "mere" citizen.

PUBLIC REACTION IS SLOW BUT DEEP

Practically all the revelations of illegal corporate payments during the 1990s, beginning with illegal campaign gifts and culminating in bribes to foreign officials, were consequences in one way or another of a single lawsuit brought by Common Cause, which forced disclosure of the secret contributors to the Nixon campaign. Once that list came into our possession, if I may quote Milton's *Paradise Lost*, Book IV, line 918, "All hell broke loose." The special prosecutor took over, the SEC moved in, the IRS and private litigants joined the pursuit. All because of one lawsuit by a group of citizens who were just stubborn enough to want to know what was going on.

In the eleven months after November 1, 1972, more than a dozen states passed major reform legislation in campaign financing, financial disclosure by public officials, lobbying disclosure, and "open meetings" laws.

The experience in Texas is particularly interesting because it illustrates the point that public reaction is slow but it runs deep. The notorious Sharpstown bank scandal in Texas broke in January 1971. It was almost a year and a half before anything approaching a significant level of public reaction manifested itself. But when the wave of revulsion came, the citizens of Texas threw out the governor, the lieutenant governor, the speaker of the House and more than half the legislature.

In early 1973, two years after the scandal broke, Common Cause members in Texas sponsored five "open government" reform bills in the Texas legislature, and all five were passed. I was in Austin the day the first bill was passed. When the news came, a senior Texan turned to me and said, "Son, you have just moved the legislature of the great state of Texas." I remember his remark not for the political compliment (which was undeserved) but because not many people called me "son" at the age of sixty-one anymore.

FOLLOWING THROUGH

With the help of a thousand volunteers throughout the country, Common Cause monitored enforcement of the new disclosure laws throughout the 1972 campaign. We uncovered widespread violations—and it came as something of a shock to the candidates to discover that someone was watching. We filed complaints against 128 Democrats and 98 Republicans.

The first deadline occurred fifteen days before the Ohio primary. We reported publicly that one of those who failed to meet the deadline was Democrat Wayne Hays, chairman of the House Administration Committee that drafted the law. Our act of public enlightenment did not gladden the heart of Representative Hays.

To do our monitoring we depended on photocopies of the reports candidates are required to submit. Within days after we had called attention to his failure to meet the filing deadline, Wayne Hays used his authority as chairman of the House Administration Committee to raise the price of copies from 10 cents to $1 a sheet—a price no citizen's group could afford to pay. We promptly went to court and brought the price down to 10 cents. The action was technically a suit against the clerk of the House of Representatives.

We set out to accomplish reform at the state level in four areas having to do with open and accountable government—campaign finance reform, lobbying disclosure, conflict-of-interest disclosure and open government. In two years, forty-two out of the fifty states passed major reforms on one or another of those issues. That was a totally unprecedented wave of reform in the states. It had never happened before in our history.

I'll leave no question unanswered, and you leave no answers unquestioned.

—Speech at Common Cause Membership Meeting, Cincinnati, 1971

The necessity for a citizen's group outside of government is obviously not understood by those who urge us to turn Common Cause into a third party. The whole point of a party is that it sets out to take over the political power hierarchy. But for those who take it over, the conventional hierarchy both empowers and imprisons. It puts you in charge but it exacts a price.

And part of the price is that you not meddle too insistently with the arrangements by which the political apparatus preserves its power. That kind of meddling is precisely what Common Cause was set up to do.

GIVING LIFE TO AN IDEA

In creating Common Cause, we have done more than create an organization. We've given life to an idea. Even if Common Cause should close its doors or lose its effectiveness some time in the twenty-first century, the idea will not die. Years later, people facing grave problems of governing will look back at Common Cause and say, "Citizens did it once. We can do it again!"

As I said in 1980 on our tenth anniversary, "The spark from one fire lights another fire, and there is a wind that blows down the path of history. The spark that we send down the wind will ignite later generations. It will not die."

PART TWO

The Courage
to Live
and Learn

4

Personal Renewal

John W. Gardner wrote in his journal: "When I speak to an audience about personal renewal, I realize that I must get through a certain amount of surface cynicism and defensiveness. But somewhere under the plodding routines of life, under the sense of defeat that they try not to think about, under the layers of self-deception and compromise and forgotten dreams is a still living, hoping, caring person who may hear me."

This speech was first given to the Twenty-Fifth Reunion Class of the Graduate School of Business at Stanford University in 1986. The class asked him to give the exact same speech five years later, at their thirtieth reunion! Variations later appeared in a number of publications and other speeches. It was widely circulated and now has a life of its own.

Not long ago, I read a splendid article on barnacles. I don't want to give the wrong impression of the focus of my reading interests. Sometimes weeks go by without my reading about barnacles, much less remembering what I read. But this article had an unforgettable opening paragraph. "The barnacle," the author explained, "is confronted with an existential decision about where it's going to live. Once it decides . . . it spends the rest of its life with its head cemented to a rock."

For a good many of us, it comes to that. A lot of people stop learning and growing far earlier than they should.

One must be compassionate in assessing the reasons. Perhaps life just presented them with tougher problems than they could solve. It happens.

41

Perhaps they were pulled down by the hidden resentments and grievances that grow in adult life, sometimes so luxuriantly that, like tangled vines, they immobilize the victim. Perhaps something inflicted a major wound on their confidence or their self-esteem. You've known such people—feeling secretly defeated, maybe somewhat sour and cynical, or perhaps just vaguely dispirited. Or perhaps they grew so comfortable that adventures no longer beckoned.

Believe me, I have the most profound respect for the blows and defeats that life can administer, and sympathy for those who have not made of their lives what they had hoped. I'm not talking about people who fail to get to the top in achievement. We can't all get to the top, and that isn't the point of life anyway. I'm talking about people who—no matter how busy they seem to be—have stopped learning or trying. Many of them are just going through the motions—and I don't deride that. Life is hard. Just to keep on keeping on is sometimes an act of courage. But I do worry about men and women at whatever age functioning below the level of their potential.

We have to face the fact that most men and women out there in the world of work are more stale than they know, more bored than they would care to admit. Boredom is one of the least celebrated of the deadly ailments. Logan Pearsall Smith said that boredom can rise to the level of a mystical experience, and if that's true I have some friends who are among the great mystics of all time. Some on university faculties. Some in high positions in corporate or public life.

We can't write off the danger of complacency, of growing rigidity, of imprisonment by our own comfortable habits and opinions. Look around you. How many people whom you know well—people even younger than yourselves—are already trapped in fixed attitudes and habits. A famous French writer said, "There are people whose clocks stop at a certain point in their lives." I could easily name a half dozen national political figures whom you would recognize, and could tell you roughly the year their clock stopped. I won't do it because I still have to deal with them occasionally.

My observations over a lifetime convince me that most people enjoy learning and growing. And many are clearly troubled by the self-assessments of midlife. Yogi Berra says you can observe a lot just by watching, and I've watched many go through those midlife assessments.

When you're young and moving up, the drama of your own rise—real or hoped for—is enough. But when you reach middle age, when your energies aren't what they used to be, you begin to wonder what it all added up to. You begin to look for the figure in the carpet of your life. I have some simple advice for you when you begin that process. Don't be too hard on yourself. Someone said that "Life is the art of drawing without an eraser." Above all don't imagine that the story is over. Life has a lot of chapters. Look ahead.

Don't succumb to the melancholy, "If I had only taken the other path!" It's a great delusion to imagine that one or two big decisions or lessons shaped your life. Thousands of decisions and lessons have shaped your life so far, and there are thousands more to come. The story is still being written.

If we are conscious of the danger of going to seed, we can resort to countervailing measures. At almost any age. You don't need to run down like an unwound clock. And if your clock is unwound, you can wind it up again. You can stay alive in every sense of the word until you fail physically. I know some people who feel that that just isn't possible for them, that life has trapped them. But they don't really know that. Life takes unexpected turns.

Renewal is in part dependent on health and physical vitality. Continued learning—lifelong learning—requires a lot of sheer physical energy. You know about the marvels of modern technology, but you may not have reflected on the fact that you will never have under your command a piece of equipment as marvelously intricate as your own physical organism. Respect it.

I said in my book *Self-Renewal* that we build our own prisons and serve as our own jailkeepers. I no longer completely agree with that. I still think we're our own jailkeepers, but clearly our parents and the society at large have a hand in building our prisons. They create roles for us—and self-images—that hold us captive for a long time. The individual intent on self-renewal will have to deal with ghosts of the past—the memory of earlier failures, the remnants of childhood dramas and rebellions, the accumulated grievances and resentments that have long outlived their cause. Sometimes people cling to the ghosts with something almost approaching pleasure—but the hampering effect on growth is inescapable. As Jim Whitaker (who climbed Mount Everest) said, "You never conquer the mountain. You only conquer yourself."

The more I see of human lives, the more I believe the business of growing up is much longer drawn out than we pretend. If we achieve it in our forties, even our fifties, we're doing well. (To those of you who are parents of teenagers, I can only say, "Sorry about that.")

There's a myth that learning is for young people. But as the proverb says, "It's what you learn after you know it all that counts." The fifties and sixties are great, great learning years. Even the years beyond that offer vivid opportunities.

Learn all your life. Learn from your failures. Learn from your successes. When you hit a spell of trouble, ask, "What is it trying to teach me?" The lessons aren't always happy ones, but they keep coming.

We learn from our jobs, from our friends and families. We learn by accepting the commitments of life, by playing the roles that life hands us (not necessarily the roles we would have chosen). We learn by growing older, by suffering, by loving, by taking risks, by bearing with the things we can't change. And what hard-won wisdom is packed into those last words, "bearing with the things we can't change"!

The things you learn in maturity aren't simple things such as acquiring information and skills. You learn not to engage in self-destructive behavior. You learn not to burn up energy in anxiety. You discover how to manage your tensions, if you have any, which you do. You learn that self-pity and resentment are among the most toxic of drugs. You find that the world loves talent but pays off on character.

You come to understand that most people are neither for you nor against you, they are thinking about themselves. You learn that no matter how hard you try to please, some people in this world are not going to love you, a lesson that is at first troubling and then really quite relaxing.

Those are things that are hard to learn early in life. As a rule you have to have picked up some mileage and some dents in your fenders before you understand. As Norman Douglas said, "There are some things you can't learn from others. You have to pass through the fire."

You come to terms with yourself. You finally grasp what S. N. Behrman meant when he said, "At the end of every road you meet yourself."

You learn the arts of mutual dependence, meeting the needs of loved ones and letting yourself need them. You can even be unaffected—a quality that often takes years to acquire. You can achieve the simplicity that lies beyond sophistication.

It's interesting that we come to understand in early childhood the impact various others have on us, but many of us are middle-aged before we begin to understand the impact we have on others—which is a pity because the impact you have on others may create the environment in which you live.

Of course, failures are a part of the story too. Everyone fails. When Joe Louis was world heavyweight boxing champion, he said, "Everyone has to figure to get beat some time." The question isn't did you fail, but did you pick yourself up and move ahead? And there is one other little question: "Did you collaborate in your own defeat?" A lot of people do. Learn not to.

The luckiest people are those who learn early, maybe in their twenties or thirties, maybe earlier, that it's essential to take charge of your own life. That doesn't mean that you don't accept help, friendship, love and leadership—if it's good leadership—from others. But it does mean recognizing that ultimately you're the one who's responsible for you. No excuses. Don't blame others. Don't blame circumstances. You take charge. And one of the things you take charge of is your own learning. It calls for character and drive.

You won't really understand the fun of learning in later years until you understand the fact of hidden possibilities. How much of your own talent and energy has been tapped? Over your whole lifetime, what fraction of your potential talent and energy will have been fully realized? I would guess that the fraction might not be higher than one half. Would you believe that one-half of what you have to give the world in talent and energy may never be tapped? You know about some of the gifts that you have left undeveloped. Would you believe that you have gifts and possibilities you don't even know about?

It is not just a matter of the ancient and familiar barriers to individual development—physical and mental ill health, poverty, ignorance, political subjugation. There are barriers that we are just beginning to understand. We are just beginning to see that the individual's potentialities may be blighted by an early environment that diminishes the sense of self-worth, by excessive pressures for conformity, by narrow specialization, by a lack of opportunities to grow. And we are just beginning to recognize how even those who have had every advantage unconsciously put a ceiling on their own growth, underestimate their potentialities or hide from the risk that growth involves.

You have to understand that the potentialities you develop to the full come as the result of an interplay between you and life's challenges—and the challenges keep coming, and they keep changing. Emergencies sometimes lead people to perform remarkable and heroic tasks that they wouldn't have guessed they were capable of. Life pulls things out of you. At least occasionally, expose yourself to unaccustomed challenges.

Learning often involves a certain amount of risk, and one of the reasons mature people learn less than young people is that they are less inclined to be risk-takers. If they are professionals or executives, proud of the disciplined skills of their field, they may be particularly wary of the floundering, groping and fumbling that goes with tackling something new. But it's the fumbling and floundering that leads to new growth. In infancy one learns more and learns it faster than at any later stage. Watch a baby learning to walk. It stands up, falls, takes a step, bumps its nose, cries and promptly tries again. It accepts the reality that risk and learning are parts of the same process.

There's something I know about you that you may or may not know about yourself. You have within you more resources of energy than have ever been tapped, more talent than has ever been exploited, more strength than has ever been tested, more to give than you have ever given.

It isn't possible to talk about renewal without touching on the subject of motivation. Someone defined horse sense as the good judgment horses have that prevents them from betting on people. But we have to bet on people—and I place my bets more often on high motivation than on any other quality except judgment. There is no perfection of techniques that will substitute for the lift of spirit and heightened performance that comes from strong motivation. The world is moved by highly motivated people, by enthusiasts, by men and women who want something very much or believe very deeply.

I'm not talking about anything as narrow as ambition. Ambition eventually wears out and probably should. But you can keep your zest until the day you die. If I may offer you a simple maxim, "Be interested." Everyone wants to be interesting—but the vitalizing thing is to be interested. Keep a sense of curiosity. Discover new things. Care. Risk failure. Reach out.

I once lived in a house where I could look out a window as I worked at my desk and observe a small herd of cattle browsing in a neighboring field. And I was struck with a thought that must have occurred to the earliest herdsmen tens of thousands of years ago. You never get the impression that a cow is about to have a nervous breakdown. Or is puzzling about the meaning of life.

Humans have never mastered that kind of complacency. We are worriers and puzzlers, and we want meaning in our lives. As Robert Louis Stevenson said, "Old or young, we're on our last cruise." We want it to mean something.

For many this life is a vale of tears; for no one is it free of pain. But we are so designed that we can cope with it if we can live in some context of meaning. Given that powerful help, we can draw on the deep springs of the human spirit to see our sorrow and suffering in the framework of all human suffering, to accept the gifts of life with thanks and endure life's indignities with dignity.

In the stable periods of history, meaning was supplied in the context of a coherent community and traditional patterns of culture. Today you can't count on any such heritage—not in this transient, rootless, pluralistic society. You have to build meaning into your life, and you build it through your commitments—whether to your religion, to an ethical order as you conceive it, to your life's work, to loved ones, to your fellow humans.

You may commit yourself to strive for certain achievements or you may commit yourself to a way of being. *There are men and women who make the world better just by being the kind of people they are.* It matters very little whether they're behind the wheel of a truck or running a corporation or bringing up a family. You know such people. The next time you see them, give them some little extra sign of respect or affection. Do it!

There's a popular view that work can't possibly be satisfying, especially hard work, because it's demanding and arduous. People are inclined to think that the purpose of our civilization is to make us "happy" and to spare us "problems." But highly motivated people have always recognized that a lot of their zest for life is linked to the tackling of problems. And that really isn't too surprising. The human organism was designed for a world in which pain, danger and the need for intense effort are realities. Humans most of the time are problem seekers. When problems don't seem readily available, we invent them. Most games are invented problems. All you have to do to convince yourself of that is to watch grown men and women chasing a little white ball around a golf course. The truth is that most human beings are so constructed that they want something active to do, something that involves not only effort but purposefulness, something that tests them, that engages their mind and their will. If they get paid for it, the world calls it "work," and they're not supposed to enjoy it. But lots of people do. It's a shocking thought, but it's true.

I'm not suggesting that you let high motivation lead you to kill yourself with work, or to neglect your families, or engage in behavior that is destructive of other values. One can become so intent as to disable oneself. Every athlete, every dancer, every musician learns that there are moments when trying too hard is counterproductive, that there is a time when one must stop straining and let the performance happen.

In life itself, there is a time to seek inner peace, a time to rid oneself of tension and anxiety. The moment comes when the striving must let up, when wisdom says, "Be quiet." You'll be surprised how the world keeps on revolving without your pushing it. And you'll be surprised how much stronger you are the next time you decide to push.

We tend to think of youth and the active middle years as the years of commitment. As you get a little older, you're told you've earned the right to think about yourself. But that's a deadly prescription! People of every age need commitments beyond the self, need the meaning that commitments provide. Self-preoccupation is a prison, as every self-absorbed person finally knows. Commitments beyond the self can get you out of prison.

Another significant ingredient in motivation is one's attitude toward the future. Optimism is unfashionable today, particularly among intellectuals. Everyone makes fun of it. Someone said, "Pessimists got that way by financing optimists." But I am not pessimistic and I advise you not to be.

For renewal, a tough-minded optimism is best. The future is not shaped by people who don't really believe in the future. Men and women of vitality have always been prepared to bet their futures, even their lives, on ventures of unknown outcome. If they had all looked before they leaped, we would still be crouched in caves sketching animal pictures on the wall.

But I did say *tough-minded* optimism. High hopes that are dashed by the first failure are precisely what we don't need. We have to believe in ourselves, but we mustn't suppose that the path will be easy. It's tough. Life is painful, and rain falls on the just; and Mr. Churchill was not being a pessimist when he said—in his country's darkest hour—"I have nothing to offer, but blood, toil, tears and sweat." He had a great deal more to offer, but as a good leader he was saying it isn't going to be easy, and he was also saying something that all great leaders say constantly—that failure is simply a reason to strengthen resolve.

We cannot dream of a Utopia in which all arrangements are ideal and everyone is flawless. Life is tumultuous—an endless losing and regaining of balance, a continuous struggle, never an assured victory. Nothing is ever finally safe. Every important battle is fought and refought. You may wonder if such a struggle—endless and of uncertain outcome—isn't more than humans can bear. But all of history suggests that the human spirit is well fitted to cope with just that kind of world.

I said earlier that life has a lot of chapters. Here is a particularly interesting true example of renewal. The man in question was fifty-three years old. Most of his adult life had been a losing struggle against debt and misfortune. In military service he received a battlefield injury that denied him the use of his left arm. And he was seized and held in captivity for five years. Later he held two government jobs, succeeding at neither. At fifty-three he was in prison—and not for the first time. There in prison, he decided to write a book, driven by Heaven knows what motive—boredom, the hope of gain, emotional release, creative impulse, who can say? And the book turned out to be one of the greatest ever written, a book that has enthralled the world for over 350 years. The prisoner was Cervantes; the book, *Don Quixote*.

Another example was Pope John XXIII, a serious man who found a lot to laugh about. The son of peasant farmers, he once said, "In Italy there are three roads to poverty—drinking, gambling and farming. My family chose the slowest of the three." When someone asked him how many people worked in the Vatican he said, "Oh, about half." He was seventy-six years old when he was elected Pope. Through a lifetime in the bureaucracy, the spark of spirit and imagination had remained undimmed, and when he reached the top he launched the most vigorous renewal that the Church had known in the twentieth century.

Still another example was Winston Churchill. At age twenty-five, as a correspondent in the Boer War, he became a prisoner of war; his dramatic escape made him a national hero. Elected to Parliament at twenty-six, he performed brilliantly, held high cabinet posts with distinction and at thirty-seven became First Lord of the Admiralty. Then he was discredited by the Dardanelles expedition—the defeat at Gallipoli—and lost his admiralty post. There followed twenty-four years of ups and downs. All too often the verdict on him was "Brilliant but erratic . . . not steady, not dependable." He had only himself to blame. A friend described him as a man who jaywalked through life. He was sixty-six before his moment of flowering came. Someone said, "It's all right to be a late bloomer if you don't miss the flower show." Churchill didn't miss it.

50

I use these examples because the names are well known to you, but I don't want to leave the impression that heroic achievement and high status are the sum of life's goals. I cite these simply as examples of irrepressible lifelong vitality.

All of my feelings about the release of human possibilities, all of my convictions about renewal, are offended by the widely shared cultural assumption that life levels off in our forties or fifties and heads downhill, so that by sixty-five we are ready for the scrap heap.

And when I detect—in people still in their forties and fifties (youngsters by my standards)—that doleful expectation of decline, it upsets me. I'm not blind to the physical problems of aging. At the age of eighty-eight, I know there are bumps in the road, some of them really bad. But what I want for those youngsters in their forties and fifties is several more decades of vital learning and growth. And I want something even broader and deeper. I don't know whether I can even put it into words. What I want for them is a long youthfulness of spirit. It doesn't sound like much to ask, but it's everything!

Life isn't a game that has a final score. Nor a riddle that has an answer. Nor a mountain that has a summit.

Life is an endless unfolding, and if we wish it to be, an endless process of self-discovery, an endless and unpredictable dialogue between our own potentialities and the life situations in which we find ourselves.

The purpose is to grow and develop in the dimensions that distinguish humankind at its best. I'm told that we will soon have robots that think in more complex ways than humans think. And that raises the question, "Are we simply organisms whose functions can be performed by thinking robots, or are we something more?"

Most of us, no doubt, are on the side of "something more"—something that springs not only from reason, or from miniaturized circuits that mimic reason, but also from the spirit, from our faith in a truth greater than ourselves, from our hopes and our tears, from the stories of the great remembered dead.

Perhaps the robots will solve the rational problems more swiftly than we. But I doubt that they will reach for unreachable stars . . . or dream impossible dreams . . . or experience what Annie Dillard calls "our complex and inexplicable caring for one another."

And that suggests a reasonable division of labor. We can work with the robots on the rational things they do so well, and we can continue on our own to bring into play other attributes—attributes that mark the species as human and may have helped it survive. I am speaking of hope, in a world that often gives little ground for hope; the insistent quest for justice in a world only fitfully committed to justice; love, in a world that is often unlovely and unloving; the hunger to understand things that elude understanding; the capacity for awe, wonder, reverence. I invite you to extend the list.

Let me tell you a story. In 1914, the fourteenth year of the incredibly dynamic and authentically terrifying twentieth century, the famous explorer Ernest Shackleton set off on an ambitious Antarctic expedition. His part of the effort ended early when his ship was crushed by pack ice. But he had already sent a team of men down to the Ross Sea (on the other side of Antarctica) to set up depots on the ice shelf that he (Shackleton) could pick up later. And in those days—before radio—there was no way for him to tell them to turn back, no way to tell them that their arduous mission was no longer necessary.

So what happened to them? When they reached Cape Evans in Antarctica, their ship was torn from its moorings, and they were left marooned.

Nevertheless, heroically, incredibly, they traveled for two seasons, through fierce blizzards and paralyzing cold, setting up the depots as Shackleton had requested, fighting hunger, fatigue, scurvy, frostbite and snow blindness. They covered two thousand miles. One died. Two set off to walk back to Cape Evans and were never seen again. It was in the words of one participant, "almost beyond human endurance," a journey that was "without parallel in the annals of polar sledging." And all to further the Shackleton expedition which had ended in disaster long before!

In his ninetieth year, one of the survivors, Dick Richards, said, "That the effort was unnecessary, that the sacrifice was made to no purpose, was in the end irrelevant. . . . I don't think of our struggle as futile. It was something that the spirit accomplished."

"Something that the spirit accomplished"! Those are not words that a robot would utter. They carry the unmistakable accent of humankind.

Many years ago I concluded a speech with a paragraph on meaning in life. The speech was reprinted over the years, and fifteen years later that final paragraph came back to me in a rather dramatic way, really a heartbreaking way.

A man wrote to me from Colorado saying that his twenty-year-old daughter had been killed in an auto accident some weeks before and that she was carrying in her billfold a paragraph from a speech of mine. He said he was grateful because the paragraph—and the fact that she kept it close to her—told him something he might not otherwise have known about her values and concerns. I can't imagine where or how she came across the paragraph, but here it is.

Meaning is not something you stumble across, like the answer to a riddle or the prize in a treasure hunt. Meaning is something you build into your life. You build it out of your own past, out of your affections and loyalties, out of the experience of humankind as it is passed on to you, out of your own talent and understanding, out of the things you believe in, out of the things and people you love, out of the values for which you are willing to sacrifice something. The ingredients are there. You are the only one who can put them together into that unique pattern that will be your life. Let it be a life that has dignity and meaning for you. If it does, then the particular balance of success or failure—as the world measures success or failure—is of less account.

5

How to Tell When You've Grown Up

After delivering more than his share of commencement speeches, in addition to advising his children, grandchildren, and innumerable young adults, John W. Gardner made a short list of criteria for assessing maturity.

It takes much longer to grow up than one might imagine. The new parental rule—"Out of the house by forty!"—is indicative. I have listed only ten of many significant criteria here. I ask readers to supply the next ten.

1. You accept responsibility. In this day of prolonged adolescence and commitment-phobia it's easy even in your thirties to believe that you're responsible to no one. It may be legal but it isn't grown up.

2. You've learned the arts of mutual dependence, learned that we achieve full humanity in a web of mutual commitments. You know how to give and receive love without exploiting those you love or are loved by. You take your turn at nurturing and let yourself need others. You recognize that all of the many kinds and varieties of loving relationships involve reaching out, accommodating, communicating, accepting vulnerability and much more.

3. You've learned that, to a considerable degree, we create our own environment. In other words, you've learned to understand your impact on others.

4. You've learned to balance your individuality and your commitments beyond the self, your self-affirmation and your obligations to the community, your independence and dependence (everyone is dependent in some dimension).

5. You have learned to deal with failure. Everyone fails. The first rule is not to collaborate in your own failure, which people do constantly. The second rule: pick yourself up and move ahead.

6. You have come to terms with the spiritual dimension of your life—though your spiritual quest may never end.

7. You forgive—partly because the great religions tell you to, and partly because grudges are an awesome waste of time and energy.

8. You recognize that you have to *be* as well as *do*—not an easy thing in a culture that puts overwhelming emphasis on performance. Some people make the world better just by being the kind of people they are. Being a serene, whole human being, in tune with the universe, one's community and oneself is a worthier goal than being Achiever of the Month.

9. You savor "the unbought grace of life." You live along the way, knowing that the path may be as important as the destination. You treasure moments—a clear morning, a friend's voice on the phone, the laughter of children (at a reasonable distance).

10. You've learned to let go, to take your hands off the world occasionally and let it spin by itself—which it does quite well. For many earnest people, inner serenity is destroyed by the obsessive need to make everything come out right. An admirable goal—but know when to let go.

6

The Fourth Maxim

> John W. Gardner was an inveterate collector of quotations, proverbs, and maxims. He loved language and well-conceived phrases in many languages. He collected them in binders and sprinkled them throughout his work. He also coedited a collection of favorites, *Quotations of Wit and Wisdom*, which has been in print for more than a quarter-century. The challenge of a One-Word Maxim intrigued him for many years.

On a quiet summer day twenty-four years ago, I began the train of thought that led eventually to the search for the Fourth Maxim.

For many years I had collected proverbs, and on that day I was thinking about the remarkable brevity of some of the greatest folk sayings.

There are many memorable ones that are no longer than four words. As every student of proverbs knows, the four-worders often rely on the use of balance, contrast and repetition: "Soon ripe, soon rotten," "Easy come, easy go," "Young saint, old sinner."

There are not so many three-word proverbs, but everyone can remember a few: "Misery loves company"; "Love is blind"; "Make haste slowly"; "Que sera, sera." Some of these are thousands of years old. If you don't find yourself impressed with that fact, try making up a three-word saying that is memorable enough to last a week.

The two-word proverbs are the aristocrats of verbal brevity, and as befits aristocrats they favor the imperative mood. There are declarative two-worders ("Power corrupts"; "Tempus fugit") but most of the two-word proverbs tell us what to do or how to live. "Know thyself" is perhaps the most famous.

As I reflected on these terse sayings I asked myself "Why not a one-word maxim?" If "Know thyself" passes muster as a legitimate maxim, why not the single word "Know"? If "Be yourself" is acceptable, why not the single word "Be"?

If you continue in that experimental vein, you soon find that the most plausible one-word maxims are verbs. There are a few nouns used in the spirit of a toast—"Health!" "Fortune!" And the nouns on coats of arms—"Honor," "Veritas." But none of these have the quality of sayings. In contrast, Harry Golden's advice "Enjoy!" seems to me a perfectly appropriate one-word maxim. And like "Know" and "Be," it is a verb in the imperative mood.

If the one-word maxim is most likely to be a verb that instructs us what to do, its value will lie entirely in the soundness of the instruction given. In longer proverbs, ideas of dubious wisdom may be saved by vividness or saltiness of expression. But in one-word proverbs vividness or any other marks of style are impossible. The value of the saying will depend entirely on the meaning of the one word.

With those thoughts firmly in mind I set out to find the choicest one-word maxims. Over weeks and months I discussed the search with many people. I put the question this way: "Suppose you were allowed to communicate one word of advice to a young person living in the year 2500. What would it be?"

One word!

The results of the conversations surprised me. It turns out that there are three one-word maxims almost universally nominated for the top of the list. There is not perfect agreement as to the order of the three, so I'll list them in the order that seems appropriate to me.

The First Maxim is "Live!" I am conscious of the moral questions the maxim may arouse (there are fates worse than death, for example), but the word—and the reality it denotes—still embraces everything else. "Live!" If you have in mind Schweitzer's "reverence for life," and a biologist's sense of the complexity and wonder of the life process, you will recognize that most people who mentioned the word had in mind more than an invitation to hedonism. Live, be, experience, grow, sense, function as a healthy organism! Everything else builds on that.

Of the three maxims most widely agreed on, another was "Learn." Learning begins before birth, and is at the heart of human behavior.

The third of the three maxims widely agreed on is "Love!" You have discovered by now that we cannot play the game of one-word maxims without allowing each maxim to carry a lot of meanings. "Love" would have to mean many kinds of love—fraternal, sexual, religious, humanistic.

So much for the first three maxims: Live, learn, love. Readers who would like to check the results with friends will find considerable agreement on those three. But when we move beyond that point, we encounter a curious fact: though people tend to agree on the first three maxims, there is nothing approaching consensus on the identity of the fourth.

A fascinating and puzzling fact!

A devout young friend of mine says, "Believe!" A scientist friend says, "Seek!" A distinguished physician, the late Dr. Russell Lee, said, "Produce!" I found no consensus.

Then some years ago I was to give an after-dinner talk to one of the most distinguished scholarly societies in the nation, and I decided to put the question to the assembled members. Where would I find a group of men and women better fitted to assist in the Search for the Fourth Maxim? I described the history of the search, and then supplied them with slips of paper on which to record their nominations.

What were the results?

If we can accept the judgment of this distinguished group, the Fourth Maxim is one or another word centering on the cognitive processes. The group was not unanimous as to what that word would be. The words most often mentioned were:

Think

Understand

Know

If one were to draw from their responses a Fifth Maxim, it would be one or another word from the following cluster:

Give
Help
Serve
Share
Care

And I'm happy to report that their Sixth Maxim would involve a lightening of the hitherto serious mood:

Laugh
Smile
Play
Enjoy

So much for the first six maxims. In my many conversations on the subject I was invariably asked, "What is your own choice for the Fourth Maxim?" My choice would be "Aspire." In some respects I would prefer the homely word "Try," but "Aspire" says more. It says "try for something better." That seems to me the essence of humans at their best.

I won't put my choice ahead of the distinguished scholars I consulted, but I'll take the liberty of ranking "Aspire" as the Seventh Maxim.

The list now goes:

Live
Learn
Love
Think
Give
Laugh
Aspire

One's preference in maxims is of course a highly personal matter. I leave it to the reader to diagnose the member of the audience who wrote on his slip of paper the word "Escape!"

Living, Leading, and the American Dream

7

Touch the Earth

"It was a hot day in August—one of those sleepy days when time stands still—or even slips back a little. My secretary came in and said that a telephone call had come in saying that I had been selected for an award because I exemplified a deep respect for nature; concern for the rights of the individual; the courage to go against the tide of public opinion; a commitment to intellectual and artistic freedom; a faith in young people; a concern for teaching and learning; and utter candor.

"I took the list as exemplifying the rhetorical license associated with awards. But then I began to get used to the idea. To imagine such splendid phrases applied to oneself is hard, but humans are amazingly well-equipped to bear that hardship. On the third reading of the list I found myself nodding in silent agreement. But the list of criteria wasn't the real excitement. The real lift was the association of the award with the name of Thomas Hart Benton. I never met Thomas Hart Benton, but I first came to know of his work in the 1930s. I read *An Artist in America* with enormous pleasure. He spoke to me. He was a man with a sense of himself and a sense of his world, his land, his talent. Reading his words and seeing his pictures provide for me two totally congruent glimpses of a whole man, an unfragmented man."

I suppose that every man or woman with the capacity to face reality, which eliminates most of us at once, recognizes that it's hard to be a whole person in today's world. It is a confusing time. Old landmarks are disappearing.

Every individual, every community, every nation is faced with torrential currents of change. No one can forgo change. The great challenge is to impose an order and direction on change that will ensure the essential continuities of spirit and character in our national life.

But that requires a sure sense of who we are—as individuals, as a people, as a nation.

Our distant forebears, distilling the wisdom of the ages as they sat by hearth and campfire, were much given to maxims, and I'm of that persuasion. And if a young person were to ask me for a dozen maxims to live by, one of them would surely be "Touch the Earth." The mythical giant Antaeus was invincible in wrestling as long as he remained in contact with his mother, Earth. Hercules vanquished him because in their wrestling match he succeeded in lifting Antaeus completely off the ground.

Antaeus is a good giant to remember in this complicated age. Contemporary life lifts us into a dizzying world of abstractions, of verbal and numerical symbols and concepts. It cuts us off from the normal cycles and rhythms of the earth and our own being. Our appetites and senses are schooled away from natural patterns. Thought and emotion are separated. The rational, technical, planful side of life is split off from the world of sensory experience and emotional release, of impulse and appetite, of fantasy and dreams (which are also of Mother Earth).

And the great exciting cosmopolitan whirl that we're all drawn into says, "Forget your roots. Be fashionable. Learn the new words and the new attitudes. Join the big world."

I've always instinctively harkened to another voice, a voice that says, "Dig your fingers into the soil. Acknowledge your roots. Know where you came from and the earth that nourished you. Know your kind of people."

Ever since the world began young people of imagination have restlessly tried on new personalities and new roles. And the fashion of the day tells them that their identity is something glamorous and unfound, something "out there," that has nothing to do with the dull old facts of their lineage, their accent, their regional style, their economic and social status, their religion; in other words, nothing to do with the realities of personal background. So they seize on fads of clothing, slang, music, manners and morals, and they imagine that those fashionable new attributes are their new identity. They are bound to believe that the new identity is more exciting than anything in their personal history.

But you will save yourself some time if you realize that you already have an extraordinarily interesting identity. It only seems dull because it's yours, and because you think you know it by heart. But there are mysteries in your biological heritage that only the years may reveal. Your cultural heritage, your ethnic background, your early surroundings, your family and family relationships are the stuff of novels, and there are hidden currents there that you can barely guess at.

The natural and common response of a young person to that kind of comment is that they are interested in the future and not the past. So am I. But the person you become will be built on the person you are. And the person you are is already more interesting and important than you know. Even if you grow far beyond your point of origin, even if you have rebelled against your background, you bear the marks of your origin and the path you have traveled. It's all a part of the same tapestry. And some figures in the tapestry—your physical and cultural heritage—are rooted in the centuries. Your immediate family, your people, the figures of your childhood are part of you, not to be rooted out. Love them if you can. If you cannot love them, endure them. If you cannot endure them, flee. But never deny them.

Understand your tradition, the ideas and beliefs and customs of your childhood and youth. They echo in your memory and will not die out. Understand your heritage, even if you rebel against it, even if you spend your life trying to alter it, even if your aversion to it drives you to the opposite end of the earth. To the extent that it lurks unacknowledged in the back corridors of your mind, you are the poorer.

Know your native corner—the place where you spent your early years. Its physical characteristics are ground deeper into your mind than you know. It is a part of you.

The aim is that you not be a person who has countless acquaintances and no witness to his or her life, who has sampled a thousand exotic ways but acknowledges no cultural roots, who has been everywhere and calls no place home. The aim is to know your distinctive lineage, the earth from which you sprang.

Then you will know your own grain—and you can sail to the ends of the earth and not be lost. Then you can love strangers and be tolerant of their beliefs. Then you can explore far places, accept alien ideas, venture into unknown territory, and the place you eventually call home may be very far from the place where you started. The people you love in the end may be very different from those with whom you began. But you will bring to that new home and those new people an authentic person.

8

The Qualities of Creativity

Creativity, as a necessary part of individual, organizational, and social self-renewal, was a constant interest. John W. Gardner saw innovation as rooted in individual achievement. His fullest discussion of innovation was found in his book *Self-Renewal,* from which this chapter is excerpted.

When we speak of the individual as a source of renewal, we call to mind the magic word *creativity*—a word of dizzying popularity at the moment. It is more than a word today; it is an incantation. People think of it as a kind of psychic wonder drug, powerful and presumably painless, and everyone wants a prescription.

It is one of our national vices to corrupt and vulgarize any word or idea that seems to have significance or relevance or freshness. And so we have done with the word creativity. But that should not lead us to neglect the idea behind the word. Granted that much of the current interest in the subject is shallow. Still it is more than a fad. It is part of a growing resistance to the tyranny of the formula, a new respect for individuality, a dawning recognition of the potentialities of the liberated mind.

We must never forget that though the word may be popular the consequences of true creativity can never be assured of popularity. New ways threaten the old, and those who are wedded to the old may prove highly intolerant. Today Galileo is a popular historical figure, and we feel wise and emancipated as we reflect indignantly on his persecution for supporting

Copernicus. But if he were to reappear today and assert something equally at odds with our own deepest beliefs, his popularity would plummet like one of those lead weights dropped from the Tower of Pisa. Our affection is generally reserved for innovators long dead.

Even Pasteur, who enjoyed as much acclaim in his lifetime as any innovator who ever lived, was the object—all his life—of bitter attack and opposition. And he understood that it was inevitable: "One day, when I was a candidate for a vacant seat at the Academy of Sciences . . . one of the oldest and most dignified members said to me, 'My friend, if they stop speaking disparagingly of you in certain journals, tell yourself that you are slipping.'"[1]

That is why innovative people often need protection. That is why a strong tradition of freedom of thought and inquiry is essential to continuous renewal.

People are not divided into two categories, those who are creative and those who are not.[2] There are degrees of the attribute. Rare are the individuals who have it in their power to achieve the highest reaches of creativity. But many can and do achieve fairly impressive levels of creativity under favorable circumstances. And quite a high proportion of the population could show some creativity some of the time in some aspect of their lives.

Popular and scientific opinion agree that the trait we are discussing is something more than intelligence alone. Each of us knows at least one brilliant individual who is essentially no more original or innovative than one of the more accomplished computers. Extensive research has demonstrated that the standardized tests of intelligence are not effective in identifying creative individuals.

Similarly, creativity requires mastery of the medium in which the work is to be done, but is something more than sheer mastery. The great artist, writer, scientist or architect has first of all mastered his craft—mastered it to the point where one might almost say that he can forget it. But not all masters of a craft are creative. The average scientist, author, artist or musician may be a solid craftsman, admirable in many ways, but not necessarily gifted with originality. In science one finds a relatively thin line of innovative individuals working at the frontier of discovery, and behind them a vast army of competent people doing routine work.

Creativity is possible in most forms of human activity. In some activities—bricklaying, let us say—the possibility is greatly limited by the nature of the task. The highest levels can be expected where performance is not severely constricted by the nature of the task to be accomplished, and in those lines of endeavor that involve man's emotions, judgment, symbolizing powers, aesthetic perceptions and spiritual impulses.

The creative process is often not responsive to conscious efforts to initiate or control it. It does not proceed methodically or in programmatic fashion. It meanders. It is unpredictable, digressive, capricious. As one scientist put it, "I can schedule my lab hours, but I can't schedule my best ideas." Obviously in any complex performance the process must at some point be brought under conscious discipline and control. But the role of the unconscious mind in creative work is clearly substantial.

Is it possible to foster creativity? The question is not easily answered. Popular books on the subject seem to be saying that the trait in question is like a muscle that profits from exercise (and the implication is that you too can bulge in the right places). Or they may take the line that creativity is a communicable secret like a golf grip or a good recipe. But research workers believe that this trait and the qualities of character, temperament and intellect that contribute to it are laid down in childhood and depend to a considerable degree on relationships within the family. We know too little about these early influences.

As far as adults are concerned, it is not certain whether anything can be done to supply creativity that is not already present. But much can be done to release the potential that is there. It is the almost universal testimony of people who possess this trait that certain kinds of environment smother their creative impulses and other kinds permit the release of these impulses.[3] The society interested in continuous renewal will strive to be a hospitable environment for the release of creativity.

When Alexander the Great visited Diogenes and asked whether he could do anything for the famed teacher, Diogenes replied, "Only stand out of my light." Perhaps some day we shall know how to heighten creativity. Until then, one of the best things we can do for creative men and women is to stand out of their light.

There are many kinds of creative individuals. Creative writers are distinguishable from creative mathematicians, and both are distinguishable from creative architects. Yet research suggests that there are traits shared by all of these and by most other highly original people.[4]

Openness. In studies of creative people one finds many references to a quality that might be described as *openness.* At one level, openness refers to the receptivity of individuals to the sights, sounds, events and ideas that impinge on them. Most of us are skillful in shutting out the world, and what we do observe we see with a jaded eye. Men or women with the gift of originality manage to keep a freshness of perception, an unspoiled awareness.

Of course this openness to experience is limited to those features of the external world that seem to individuals to be relevant to their inner lives. No one could be indiscriminately open to all the clutter and clatter of life. Creative individuals achieve their heightened awareness of some aspects of life by ignoring other aspects. And since the aspects they ignore are often precisely those conventional matters on which the rest of us lavish loving attention, they are often put down as odd.

More significant than their receptivity to the external world is their exceptional openness to their own inner life. They do not suppress or refuse to face their own emotions, anxieties and fantasies. In more technical terms, MacKinnon and his associates say that creative persons are better able "to relinquish conscious control and to face without fear and anxiety the impulses and imagery arising from more primitive and unconscious layers of the personality."[5] They have fewer internal barriers or watertight compartments of experience. They are self-understanding, self-accepting.

The significance of this openness to one's own inner experience is obvious in the case of creative writers. As a result of it, they have access to the full richness of one person's emotional, spiritual and intellectual experience. But the trait can be relevant even in the cases of people who appear to be dealing wholly with the external world. Creative engineers let their hunches and wild ideas come to the surface, whereas the uncreative ones would tend to censor them.

Independence. Creative individuals have the capacity to free themselves from the web of social pressures in which the rest of us are caught. They don't spend much time asking "What will people say?" The fact that "everybody's doing it" doesn't mean they're doing it. They question assumptions that the rest of us accept. As J. P. Guilford has pointed out, they are particularly gifted in seeing the gap between what is and what *could be* (which means, of course, that they have achieved a certain measure of detachment from what *is*).[6]

It is easy to fall into romantic exaggeration in speaking of the capacity of people of originality to stand apart. Those who are responsible for the great innovative performances have always built on the work of others, and have enjoyed many kinds of social support, stimulation and communication. They are independent but they are not adrift.

The independence or detachment of creative individuals is at the heart of their capacity to take risks and to expose themselves to the probability of criticism from their fellows. Does this mean that they are nonconformists? Yes, but not necessarily in the popular sense of the word. One of the interesting findings contained in recent research is that creative individuals as a rule choose to conform in the routine, everyday matters of life, such as speech, dress, and manners. One gets the impression that they are simply not prepared to waste their energy in nonconformity about trifles. They reserve their independence for what really concerns them, the area in which their creative activities occur. This distinguishes them sharply from the exhibitionists who reject convention in those matters that will gain the most attention.

Flexibility. Still another widely observed trait may be labeled *flexibility.* It is perhaps best seen in what has been called the playfulness of persons of originality. They will toy with an idea, try it on for size, look at it from a dozen different angles, argue to themselves that it is true and then argue that it is untrue. Unlike the rest of us, they do not persist stubbornly in one approach to a problem. They can change directions and shift strategies. They can give up their initial perception of a problem and redefine it.

An even more important ingredient in their flexibility is their capacity to maintain a certain detachment from the conventional categories and abstractions that people use, and a similar detachment from the routines and fixed customs of those around them. They even manage to exercise a reasonable detachment from their own past attitudes and habits of mind, their own pet categories. (In the current fashion we talk much of the limitations on freedom that result from outside pressures and tend to forget the limitations imposed by one's own compulsions, neuroticisms, habits and fixed ideas.)

Related to this flexibility is a trait of the creative person that psychologists have called a "tolerance for ambiguity." These individuals have a capacity to tolerate internal conflict, a willingness to suspend judgment. They are not uncomfortable in the presence of unanswered questions or unresolved differences. They do not find it difficult to give expression to opposite sides of their nature at the same time—conscious and unconscious mind, reason and passion, aesthetic and scientific impulses.

Some observers have been led to comment on a certain "childlike" or "primitive" quality in creative individuals. They are childlike and primitive in the sense that they have not been trapped by the learned rigidities that immobilize the rest of us. In their chosen field they do not have the brittle knowingness and sophistication of people who think they know all the answers. The advantage of this fluidity is that it permits all kinds of combinations and recombinations of experience with a minimum of rigidity.

Capacity to find order in experience. The individual of high originality, having opened himself to such a rich and varied range of experience, exhibits an extraordinary capacity to find the order that underlies that varied experience, I would even say an extraordinary capacity to *impose* order on experience. And, as MacKinnon has suggested, it may be that the creative individual could not tolerate such a wild profusion of ideas and experiences if he did not have profound confidence in his capacity to bring some new kind of order out of this chaos.

This aspect of the creative process has not received the emphasis it deserves. We have made much of the fact that innovators free themselves from old patterns and have neglected to emphasize that they do so in order to forge new patterns. This, if you reflect on it, suggests a picture of the creative individual fundamentally different from the romanticized version. The portraits in popular literature of artists or other creative persons have all too frequently led us to suppose that people of high originality are somehow lawless. The truly creative person is not an outlaw but a lawmaker. Every great creative performance since the initial one has been in some measure a bringing of order out of chaos. It brings about a new relatedness, connects things that did not previously seem connected, sketches a more embracing framework, moves toward larger and more inclusive understandings.

One could list a number of other traits that have been ascribed to the creative individual by research workers. Almost all observers have noted a remarkable zeal or drive in creative individuals. They are wholly absorbed in their work. Anne Roe, in her study of gifted scientists, found that one of their most striking traits was a willingness to work hard and for long hours.[7] The energy they bring to their work is not only intense but sustained. Most of the great creative performances grow out of years of arduous application.

Other observers have commented on the confidence, self-assertiveness or, as one investigator put it, the "sense of destiny" in creative persons. They have faith in their capacity to do the things they want and need to do in the area of their chosen work.

PART THREE

The Release of Human Possibilities

9

Commitment and Meaning

The quest for meaning is as old as history and a central theme in all great literature. For John W. Gardner the meaning of life is largely found in the commitments one makes to something beyond the self. This discussion of meaning and commitment is taken from his book *Self-Renewal*.

In maturity one undertakes commitments to something larger than the service of one's "convulsive little ego," to use William James's memorable phrase—religious commitments, commitments to loved ones, to the social enterprise and to the moral order. In a free society we shall never specify too closely what those commitments should be.

Young people today would have a far easier time understanding the role of commitment in their lives if they were not misled by the juvenile interpretation of the "pursuit of happiness" that is widely held today. It is not unduly harsh to say that the contemporary idea of happiness cannot possibly be taken seriously by anyone whose intellectual or moral development has progressed beyond that of a three-week-old puppy. From Aristotle to Jefferson, philosophers who have thought seriously about happiness would be startled to discover how that word is now interpreted.

The truth is that few humans are capable of achieving the vegetative state implied in the current conception of happiness. Despite almost universal belief to the contrary, gratification, ease, comfort, diversion and a state of having achieved all one's goals do not constitute happiness for humans. The reason Americans have not trapped the bluebird of happiness, despite the most frantic efforts the world has ever seen, is that happiness as total gratification is not a state to which we can aspire. The irony is that we should have brought such unprecedented dynamism to the search for such a static condition.

The American commitment is not to affluence, nor to all the cushioned comforts of a well-fed nation, but to the liberation of the human spirit, the release of human potential, the enhancement of individual dignity. Those are the great themes of our life as a people. Everything else is a means to those ends.

Some of our fellow citizens do not honor those ends. But many live by the American commitment and live to further that commitment. They come from all walks of life. They constitute the brotherhood and sisterhood of those who care enough about the American commitment to do something about it. It is an army without banners, and its campaigns are not reported on the front page—but it is marching.

Every time a teacher strives to give honest individual attention to a child, she is advancing the cause. Every time an employer seeks to create the working environment in which individual employees can flourish and grow, he is helping. So is every mother who provides the special combination of love and instruction that makes for early emergence of a sense of responsibility.

Anyone can contribute and I count the contribution as a measure of those I meet. I don't want to know what their religion is or their political party, or the size of their bankroll. I want to know what they have done lately about the American commitment.

—Speech at Education Symposium, University of Texas, Austin, 1972

It might be possible for an impoverished nation to harbor the delusion that happiness is simply comfort and pleasure and having enough of everything. But we have tried it, and we know better.

One can accept this fact without at the same time underrating the pleasant things in life. One is rightly suspicious of those who tell poor people that they should be content with poverty, or hungry people that hunger is ennobling. Every human being should have the chance to enjoy the comforts and pleasures of good living. All we are saying here is that they are not enough. If they were, the large number of Americans who have been able to indulge their whims on a scale unprecedented in history would be deliriously happy. They would be telling one another of their unparalleled serenity and bliss instead of trading tranquilizer prescriptions.

So we are coming to a conception of happiness that differs fundamentally from the storybook version. The storybook conception tells of desires fulfilled; the truer version involves striving toward meaningful goals—goals that relate the individual to a larger context of purposes. Storybook happiness involves a bland idleness; the truer conception involves seeking and purposeful effort. Storybook happiness involves every form of pleasant thumb-twiddling; true happiness involves the full use of one's powers and talents. Both conceptions of happiness involve love, but the storybook version puts great emphasis on being loved, the truer version more emphasis on the capacity to give love.

This more mature and meaningful view opens up the possibility that one might even achieve happiness in striving to meet one's moral responsibilities, an outcome that is most unlikely under the present view unless one's moral responsibilities happen to be uncommonly diverting.

Note that we speak of happiness as involving a "striving toward" significant goals, not necessarily the attaining of those goals. It is characteristic of some kinds of human striving that the goals may be unattainable. Those who dedicate their lives to the achieving of good government or to the combating of human misery may enjoy small victories but they can never win the longer battle. The goal recedes before them. Such striving, says Allport, "confers unity upon personality, but it is never the unity of fulfillment, of repose, or of reduced tension."[1]

For this reason, self-renewing people never feel that they have "arrived." They know that the really important tasks are never finished—interrupted, perhaps, but never finished and all the significant goals recede before one. Those who think that they have arrived have simply lost sight of those goals (or perhaps never saw them in the first place).

Don't pray for the day when we finally solve our problems. Pray for freedom to continue working on the problems the future will never cease to throw at us.

—Journals

It is widely believed that humans in their natural state will do only what is required to achieve strictly physical satisfactions, but as every anthropologist can testify, this is not true. Primitives are intensely committed to their social group and to the moral order as they conceive it. One has to be fairly well steeped in the artificialities of civilization before one can imagine that indulgence of physical satisfactions might be a complete way of life.

Anyone can see that most men and women are quite prepared to (and do) undergo hardship and suffering in behalf of a significant goal. Indeed, they often actually court hardship in behalf of something they believe in. "Virtue will have naught to do with ease," wrote Montaigne. "It seeks a rough and thorny path."[2]

This is not to say that the aims that humans conceive beyond the needs of the self are necessarily ones that would win our admiration. They may be expressions of the highest idealism or they may be crude, even vicious. That is a salient feature of the problem. If we make the mistake of imagining that only the material wants of people need be satisfied and offer them no significant meanings, they are likely to seize upon the first "meanings" that present themselves, however shallow and foolish, committing themselves to false gods, to irrational political movements, to cults and to fads. It is essential that the human hunger for dedication find worthy objects.

Living, Leading, and the American Dream

It would be wrong to leave the implication that we are selfless creatures who only wish to place ourselves at the service of some higher ideal. Having rejected the oversimplified view of our nature as wholly materialistic and selfish, we must not fall into the opposite error. Humans are complex and contradictory beings, egocentric but inescapably involved with their fellow beings, selfish but capable of superb selflessness. We are preoccupied with our own needs, yet we find no meaning in life unless we relate ourselves to something more comprehensive than those needs. It is the tension between our egocentrism and our social and moral leanings that has produced much of the drama in human history.

Of course one always thinks one's neighbor should be more dedicated. Our own passion for dedication is contaminated by selfishness, laziness, and inconstancy, but our ardor for the other fellow's dedication is pure and undefiled. The employer believes that employees should be more dedicated to their work (meaning usually that they should work harder for less pay). Older people think young people should be more dedicated. We are all familiar with the moral zeal that rises in our breast when we think of the standards the other fellow ought to live up to. Artemus Ward said, "I have already given two cousins to the war, and I stand ready to sacrifice my wife's brother. . . ."

Nothing that is said here should be taken as an encouragement of such vicarious morality. Nor is anything that we say here to be taken as a defense of other misguided forms of commitment. There will never be a way of preventing fools from dedicating themselves to silly causes. There is no way to save some intense and unstable minds from a style of dedication that is in fact fanaticism.

Aside from these obvious dangers, there are other more subtle hazards in dedication. Anyone who thinks, for example, that a determination to "do good to others" is not accompanied by certain hazards should remember Thoreau's comment: "If I knew . . . that a man was coming to my house with the conscious design of doing me good, I should run for my life."[3] Doing good to others may be an expression of the purest altruism or it may simply be a means of demonstrating one's superiority or of living vicariously.

HUNGER FOR MEANING

Humans are in their nature seekers of meaning. They cannot help being so any more than they can help breathing or maintaining a certain body temperature. It is the way their central nervous systems work.

In most societies and most ages, however primitive they may have been technologically, the hunger for meaning was amply served. Though some of the religions, mythologies, and tribal superstitions with which the hunger for meaning was fed were crude and impoverished, they did purport to describe a larger framework in terms of which one's life gained significance.

With the arrival of the modern age a good many misguided souls conceived the notion that we could do without such nourishment. And for a breath-taking moment it did seem possible, in view of the glittering promises that modern life offered. Under the banner of a beneficial modernity, the individual was to have security, money, power, sensual gratification and status as high as anyone. He would be a solvent and eupeptic Walter Mitty in a rich and meaningless world.

But even (or especially) those who came close to achieving the dream never got over the nagging hunger for meaning.

At one level, our search for meanings is objectively intellectual. We strive to organize what we know into coherent patterns. Studies of perception have demonstrated that this tendency to organize experience is not an afterthought or the result of conscious impulse but an integral feature of the perceptual process. At the level of ideas, our inclination to organize meaningful wholes out of our experience is equally demonstrable. We try to reduce the stream of experience to orderly sequences and patterns. We produce legends, theories, philosophies.

To an impressive degree, the theories of nature and the universe that we have developed are impersonal in the sense that they take no special account of our own aspirations and status (though they are strictly dependent on our conceptualizing power and rarely wholly divorced from our values). Out of this impersonal search for meaning has come modern science.

But we have never been satisfied to let it go at that. We have throughout history shown a compelling need to arrive at conceptions of the universe in *terms of which we could regard our own lives as meaningful.* We want to know where *we* fit into the scheme of things. We want to understand how the great facts of the objective world relate to us and what they imply for our behavior. We want to know what significance may be found in our own existence, the succeeding generations of our kind and the vivid events of our inner life. We seek some kind of meaningful framework in which to understand (or at least to reconcile ourselves to) the indignities of chance and circumstance and the fact of death. A number of philosophers and scientists have told us sternly that we must not expect answers to that sort of question, but we pay little heed. We want, in the words of Kierkegaard, "a truth that is true for me."[4] We seek conceptions of the universe that give dignity, purpose and sense to our own existence.

When we fail in this effort we exhibit what Tillich describes as the anxiety of meaninglessness—"anxiety about the loss of an ultimate concern, of a meaning which gives meaning to all meanings."[5] As Erikson has pointed out, the young person's search for identity is in some respects this sort of search for meaning.[6] It is a search for a framework in terms of which young persons may understand their own aims, their relation to their fellow beings and their relation to larger purposes. In our society every individual is free to conduct this search on his own terms and to find, if he is lucky, the answer that is right for him.

MEANING, PURPOSE, AND COMMITMENT

There are those who think of the meaning of life as resembling the answer to a riddle. One searches for years, and then some bright day one finds it, like the prize at the end of a treasure hunt. This is a profoundly misleading notion. The meanings in any life are multiple and varied. Some are grasped very early, some late; some have a heavy emotional component, some are strictly intellectual; some merit the label religious, some are better described as social. But each kind of meaning implies a relationship between the person and some larger system of ideas or values, a relationship involving obligations as well as rewards. In the individual life, meaning, purpose and commitment are inseparable. When one succeeds in the search for identity one has found the answer not only to the question "Who am I" but to a lot of other questions too: "What must I live up to? What are my obligations? To what must I commit myself?"

A free society will not specify too closely the kinds of meaning different individuals will find or the things about which they should generate conviction. People differ in their goals and convictions and in the whole style of their commitment. We must ask that their goals fall within the moral framework to which we all pay allegiance, but we cannot prescribe the things that will unlock their deepest motivations. Those earnest spirits who believe that one cannot be counted worthy unless one burns with zeal for civic affairs could not be more misguided. And we are wrong when we follow the current fashion of identifying moral strength too exclusively with fighting for a cause. Nothing could be more admirable nor more appealing to us as a performance-minded people. But such an emphasis hardly does justice to the rich variety of moral excellences that humans have sought and occasionally achieved in the course of history.

> For men and women who have accepted the reality of change, the need for endless learning and trying is a way of living, a way of thinking, a way of being awake and ready. Life isn't a train ride where you choose your destination, pay your fare and settle back for a nap. It's a cycle ride over uncertain terrain, with you in the cyclist's seat, constantly correcting your balance and determining the direction of progress. It's difficult, sometimes profoundly painful. But it's better than napping through life.
>
> —*Self-Renewal* (Rev. ed.), 1981, p. xii

A good many of the most valuable people in any society will never burn with zeal for anything except the integrity and health and well-being of their own families—and if they achieve those goals, we need ask little more of

them. There are other valuable members of a society who will never generate conviction about anything beyond the productive output of their hands
or minds—and a sensible society will be grateful for their contributions.
Nor will it be too quick to define some callings as noble and some as ordinary. One may not quite accept Oliver Wendell Holmes's dictum—"Every
calling is great when greatly pursued"[7]—but the grain of truth is there.

Motivation and the Triumphant Expression of Talent

"There is nothing more essential to the dynamism of a social system than the effectiveness and capacity, the quality and vitality of the human beings in the system. The greatest asset of any society is the talent and energy of its people. Yet no society has ever fully recognized or honored that asset; indeed, most societies have effectively stifled both talent and energy." So John W. Gardner wrote in his journal. In this selection from *Excellence* he discusses the ways to motivate individuals to keep themselves and their society vital and free.

It is essential to a society's health—obviously—that people have confidence in their institutions. But they don't need to believe that their society is perfect. Far from it. They need to believe that on balance it is likely to meet their basic needs and confirm their values—or that it is moving toward meeting needs and confirming values. Humans have always lived partly on present satisfaction, partly on hope. And it's the task of the leader to keep hope alive. It is the ultimate fuel.

Psychologists have ways of measuring what individuals think is possible as a result of their own intentional behavior. Attitudes range from total fatalism ("Everything is determined by forces outside myself") to total confidence in one's own control of events. It should come as no surprise to learn that individuals from impoverished populations tend to be bunched at the fatalistic end of the scale, and unfortunately the lack of belief that any act of theirs will better their lives leads all too often to a deadening passivity.

I was talking once with a farmhand in Venezuela who was working on a rather promising experimental farm, and I asked him if he thought the experiment would prove beneficial. He said, "I think maybe it will benefit somebody, but it will not benefit me or my people. For us, nothing ever changes."

One must pause to reflect on the depth of subjugation reflected in that remark. The final stage of subjugation is the extinction of hope. The oppression experienced by those who fear machine guns and manacles is shallow compared to the oppression suffered by those who, over generations, are finally completely subjugated by their own lack of hope.

I cite the extreme case to dramatize the point, but the problem in more moderate forms is known to every teacher and leader.

In 1967 I had a conversation with Martin Luther King Jr. at an educational conference. A black woman had just presented a paper titled, if I remember correctly, "First, Teach Them to Read." King leaned over to me and said, "First, teach them to believe in themselves." Strictly speaking, of course, she could teach them to believe in themselves while teaching them to read. But King was making an important point. Any leader, any athletic coach, any teacher, any counselor, understands.

Creativity within an organization or society is to be found among men and women who are far removed from the fatalistic end of the scale. They have a powerful conviction that they can affect events in some measure. Leaders at every level must help their people keep that belief. There are all too many factors in contemporary life that diminish it.

An obstacle to sound motivation and morale is the Utopianism which says that humans and their societies are perfectible, that we can, if we're smart, figure out the perfect state of things and achieve it. Then we can all relax. Life in a hammock. People who hold that view are then very disappointed when we don't achieve the perfect state of things. They tried hard, they were bright, and their intentions were good—and yet problems remain. Is there no rest for the weary? As a matter of fact, there isn't. It's an endless struggle, and humans, contrary to popular myth, are well fitted for that endless struggle.

CHALLENGE AND RESPONSE

Good teachers and good leaders share a bit of knowledge that is not universally recognized. They know that if they expect a lot of their respective constituencies, they increase the likelihood of high performance. A teacher of handicapped children said to me, "It's a sin to ask too little of these children. If we ask too little of them, they'll ask too little of themselves. They have to ask a lot of themselves."

"Expect a lot, get a lot." That means standards, an explicit regard for excellence. In a high-morale society, people expect a lot of one another, hold one another to high standards. And leaders play a special role in conveying such expectations. Good leaders don't ask more than their constituents can give, but they often ask—and get—more than their constituents intended to give or thought it was possible to give.

Every emergency, every crisis reveals unsuspected resources of personal strength in some people and evokes heightened motivation in almost all. In speaking of the hero born of such a crisis, people say, "I didn't know he had it in him." But most of us have, in fact, a better, stouter-hearted, more vigorous self within us—a self that's deliberately a little hard of hearing but by no means stone deaf.

We all know that some organizations, some families, some athletic teams, some political groups inspire their members to great heights of personal performance. In other words, high individual performance will depend to some extent on the capacity of the society or institution to evoke it.

When an institution, organization, or nation loses its capacity to inspire high individual performance, its great days are over.

Many factors contribute to the rise of a civilization—accidents of resource availability, geographical considerations, preeminence in trade or military power. But whatever the other ingredients, a civilization rises to greatness when something happens in human minds. There occurs at breathtaking moments in history an exhilarating burst of energy and motivation, of hope and zest and imagination, and a severing of the bonds that normally hold in check the full release of human possibilities. A door is opened and the caged eagle soars.

—*On Leadership*, 1990, p. 193

We are beginning to understand that the various kinds of talents that flower in any society are the kinds that are valued in the society. On a visit to Holland, my wife asked our hostess why children and adults in that country showed such an extraordinarily high incidence of language skills. "We expect it of children," the woman said simply. "We think it important." High performance takes place in a framework of expectation.

The fact has implications far beyond education. It means that, as a society, we shall have only the kinds of talent we nourish, only the kinds of talent we want and expect. Are we nourishing the kinds of talent that will create a great civilization? In matters relating to talent and society that is not just another question. It is The Question.

One difficulty is that we shall get more or less precisely what we deserve. We cannot worship frivolity and expect our young people to scorn it. We cannot scorn the life of the mind and expect our young people to honor it. H. W. Shaw said, "To bring up a child in the way he should go, travel that way yourself once in a while."[1] Our children will respect learning if their elders respect learning. They will value the things of the mind and spirit if the society values them.

But though the child is indirectly influenced by these broader attitudes in the society as a whole, his growth depends more directly on the character of his own immediate world—his family and neighborhood. If this small world has the power to nourish and challenge his mind and spirit, the shortcomings of the larger society matter little. Thus in an earlier generation, even in the bleakest frontier community a youngster might be inspired to a lifetime of learning by parents who cared about his education.

For adults, leaders have a major responsibility in establishing the framework of expectation.

EXPECTATION AND FAITH

Let me broaden the point and express it in another way. Good leaders and good teachers, as our culture measures goodness in those callings, must have a positive view of what can be accomplished.

Obviously optimism can be carried to the point of foolishness. Churchill was a master at building the British people's confidence in themselves, but he understood that optimism must be tempered with realism. He said, "I have nothing to offer but blood, toil, tears and sweat." He had, in fact, a great deal more to offer, but he was saying that it wasn't going to be easy. He was saying what all leaders sooner or later find themselves saying—that failure is simply a reason to strengthen resolve.

Much of human performance is conditioned by what the performer thinks is possible for him. Leaders understand that. There was a time when people thought it was physically impossible to run a four-minute mile. When Roger Bannister ran it in under four minutes, he broke the physical barrier and the mental barrier as well. Two other runners accomplished the feat in a matter of weeks.

William James said, "Just as our courage is often a reflex of someone else's courage, so our faith is often a faith in someone else's faith." If you believe in me, it's easier for me to believe in myself.

In leading, in teaching, in dealing with young people, in all relationships of influencing, directing, guiding, helping, nurturing, the whole tone of the relationship will be conditioned by our faith in human possibilities. That is the generative element, the source of the current that runs beneath the surface of such relationships.

> The longer I live, the more I respect enthusiasm. There is no perfection of technique that will substitute for the lift of spirit that enthusiasm produces. Some people keep their zest until the day they die. They keep a sense of curiosity. They care about things. They reach out. They enjoy. They risk failure. They may even allow themselves some moderately cheerful expectations for the time ahead. Such expectations may be greeted with skepticism in the current climate, but we should welcome the buoyancy from which they spring. Otherwise, in our-world-weary wisdom, we shall be unresponsive to challenges that keep societies alive and moving.
>
> —*Morale*, 1978, p. 62

To conclude this discussion, I ask readers to renew their acquaintance with a leader who understood all of these considerations out of the depths of his own being. I urge readers, on their next visit to Washington, to find their way down to the western end of the Mall and revisit the Lincoln Memorial. It will be essential, of course, to take some time to study the face of Lincoln. Few images are more deeply etched in our minds and memories—and in a nation virtually without icons, few images are so closely associated with our sense of ourselves as a people.

He is the president who touched our souls. On one hand he was the homespun, rather awkward man who said, "I have endured a great deal of ridicule without much malice, and have received a great deal of kindness not quite free from ridicule," and on the other hand he was the great leader-teacher whose heart-piercing words are inscribed on the north and south walls of the Memorial. I won't quote them here. Go read them.

To select, not at random, one of Lincoln's great qualities, he had faith in the people of this country. In the conventional model, people want to know whether the followers believe in the leader. I want to know whether the leader believes in the followers.

If our leaders at all levels are to be capable of lifting us and moving us toward excellence, they are going to have to believe in the people of this nation—a people able to perform splendidly and inclined to perform indifferently, a people deeply troubled in their efforts to find a future worthy of their past, a people capable of greatness and desperately in need of encouragement to achieve that greatness.

11

The Full Expression of Human Excellence

The subject of excellence "has never ceased to interest me," John W. Gardner writes in this selection from his first book, which is simply titled *Excellence.* He did not think that excellence was a simple quality one could go in search of.

In the 1930s, Senator Huey Long, "The Kingfish," set new standards of demagoguery in this country with his slogans "Every Man a King" and "Share the Wealth." The phrases were politically potent for Long's constituency, but also widely parroted in a humorous way. So it did not surprise me when, as a young professor, I encountered them one day in altered form on the blackboard of my classroom. It was the day of the final exam, and someone had scrawled on the board "Every Man an A Student!" and below it "Share the Grades!"

It was all in fun, and the culprit turned out to be one of my best students. But the phrases ground themselves into my mind. Lurking behind the words were some interesting social meanings. It was not hard to detect in the educational world of the 1930s echoes of the same equalitarianism that rang in those phrases.

The subject has never ceased to interest me. Excellence, more particularly the conditions under which excellence is possible in our kind of society; but also—inevitably—equality, the kinds of equality that can and must be honored, and the kinds that cannot be forced. It raises some questions which Americans have shown little inclination to discuss rationally.

- What are the characteristic difficulties a democracy encounters in pursuing excellence? Is there a way out of these difficulties?
- How equal do we want to be? How equal can we be?
- What do we mean when we say, "Let the best man win"? Can an equalitarian society tolerate winners?
- Are we overproducing highly educated people? How much talent can the society absorb? Does society owe a living to talent? Does talent invariably have a chance to exhibit itself in our society?
- Does every young American have a "right" to a college education?
- Are we headed toward domination by an intellectual elite?
- Is it possible for a people to achieve excellence if they don't believe in anything? Have the American people lost their sense of purpose and the drive which would make it possible for them to achieve excellence?

I have discussed these matters with a great variety of individuals and groups throughout the country, and I find that *excellence* is a curiously powerful word—a word about which people feel strongly and deeply. But it is a word that means different things to different people. It is a little like those ink blots that psychologists use to interpret personality. As the individual contemplates the word *excellence* he reads into it his own aspirations, his own conception of high standards, his hopes for a better world. And it brings powerfully to his mind evidence of the betrayal of excellence (as he conceives it). He thinks not only of the greatness we might achieve but of the mediocrity we have fallen into.

These highly individual reactions to the word excellence create difficulties for the writer or speaker concerned with the subject. When one has had his say, someone is certain to mutter, "How could he talk about excellence without mentioning the Greeks?" And another, "He didn't say a word about the plight of the artist" . . . "Nor teachers' salaries" . . . "Nor the organization man!"

It isn't just that people have different opinions about excellence. They see it from different vantage points. The elementary school teacher preoccupied with instilling respect for standards in seven-year-olds will think about it in one way. The literary critic concerned with understanding and interpreting the highest reaches of creative expression will think of it in a wholly different way. The statesman, the composer, the intellectual historian—each will raise his own questions and pose the issues which are important for him.

I am concerned with the social context in which excellence may survive or be smothered. I am concerned with the fate of excellence in our kind of society. This is not Utopian. Some of those who complain about the quality of our national life seem to be dreaming of a world in which everyone without exception has talent, taste, judgment and an unswerving allegiance to excellence. Such dreams are pleasant but unprofitable. The problem is to achieve some measure of excellence in this society, with all its beloved and exasperating clutter, with all its exciting and debilitating confusion of standards, with all the stubborn problems that won't be solved and the equally stubborn ones that might be.

THE MANY KINDS OF EXCELLENCE

That there are many varieties of excellence is a truth of which we must continually remind ourselves. The Duke of Wellington, in a famous incident, revealed an enviable understanding of it. The government was considering the dispatch of an expedition to Burma to take Rangoon. The Cabinet summoned Wellington and asked him who would be the ablest general to head such an undertaking. He said, "Send Lord Combermere." The government officials protested: "But we have always understood that Your Grace thought Lord Combermere a fool." The duke's response was vigorous and to the point. "So he is a fool, and a damned fool, but he can take Rangoon."[1]

In intellectual fields alone there are many kinds of excellence. There is the kind of intellectual activity that leads to a new theory and the kind that leads to a new machine. There is the mind that finds its most effective expression in teaching and the mind that is most at home in research. There is the mind that works best in quantitative terms and the mind that luxuriates in poetic imagery.

There is excellence in art, in music, in craftsmanship, in human relations, in technical work, in leadership, in parental responsibilities. There are those who perform great deeds and those who make it possible for others to perform great deeds. There are pathfinders and path preservers. There are those who nurture and those who inspire. There are those whose excellence involves doing something well and those whose excellence lies in being the kind of people they are, lies in their kindness or honesty or courage.

There are kinds of excellence (such as athletics) in which a scoreboard is essential and kinds of excellence so subjective that the world cannot even observe much less appraise them. Montaigne wrote, "It is not only for an exterior show or ostentation that our soul must play her part, but inwardly within ourselves, where no eyes shine but ours."

There is a way of measuring excellence that involves comparison between people—some are musical geniuses and some are not; and there is another that involves comparison between myself at my best and myself at my worst. It is this latter comparison which enables me to assert that I am being true to the best that is in me—or forces me to confess that I am not.

Definitions of excellence tend to be most narrow at the point where we are selecting individuals, or testing them, or training them. In the course of daily life, mature people recognize many varieties of excellence in one another. But when we are selecting, testing, or training we arbitrarily narrow the range. The reasons for doing so are practical ones. To the extent that we admit a great variety of kinds of excellence we make the task of selection more difficult. Narrowing the grounds for selection is one way of making the selection process manageable—but the narrowing may do a grave injustice to those whose dimensions of excellence fall outside the narrow range.

Self-doubt undermines the possibility of high performance without leaving a fingerprint.

—Journals

Consider the relatively narrow bottleneck through which most young-sters enter a career as a scientist. What they need to pass through that bottle-neck is the capacity to manipulate abstract symbols and to give the kind of intellectual response required on intelligence or achievement tests. This ca-pacity for abstract reasoning and for dealing with mathematical and verbal symbols is useful not only on the tests but in every course they take. There are other factors that contribute to success in graduate school, but most graduate students would agree that this is the heart and soul of the matter.

On the other hand, if one looks at a group of mature scientists—in their fifties, let us say—one finds that those who are respected have arrived at their high station by a remarkable variety of routes. A small proportion of the very bright ones have the special dimension of creativity that brings historic advances in their field. Others are honored for their extraordinary gifts as teachers: their students are their great contribution to the world. Others are respected—though perhaps not loved—for their devastating critical faculties. And so the list goes. Some are specialists by nature, some generalists; some creative, some plodding; some gifted in action, some in expression.

If we reflect on the way in which we judge our own contemporaries we will recognize the varied standards of judgment that come into play. But though in daily life we recognize a good many kinds of high performance, the range is still narrower than it should be. One way to make ourselves see this is to reflect on the diverse kinds of excellence that human beings have honored at different times and places. At any given time in a particular so-ciety, the idea of what constitutes excellence tends to be limited—but the conception changes as we move from one society to another or one century to another. Baltasar Gracian said: "It is not everyone that finds the age he deserves. . . . Some men have been worthy of a better century, for every species of good does not triumph. Things have their period; even excellences are subject to fashion."[2]

Taking the whole span of history and literature, the images of excellence are amply varied: Confucius teaching the feudal lords to govern wisely . . . Leonidas defending the pass at Thermopylae . . . Saint Francis preaching to the birds at Alviano . . . Lincoln writing the Second Inaugural "with malice toward none" ... Mozart composing his first oratorio at the age of eleven ... Kepler calculating the planetary orbits ... Emily Dickinson jotting her "letters to the world" on scraps of paper ... Jesus saying, "Father, forgive them; for they know not what they do" ... Florence Nightingale nursing the wounded at Balaclava ... Eli Whitney pioneering the manufacture of interchangeable parts ... Ruth saying to Naomi, "Thy people shall be my people."

The list is long and the variety is great. Taken collectively, human societies have gone a long way toward exploring the full range of human excellences. But a particular society at a given moment in history is apt to honor only a portion of the full range. And wise indeed is the society that is not afraid to face hard questions about its own practices on this point. Is it honoring the excellences that are likely to be most fruitful for its own continued vitality? To what excellences is it relatively insensitive—and what does this imply for the tone and texture of its life? Is it squandering approbation on kinds of high performance that have nothing to contribute to its creativity as a society?

Those who can contemplate those questions without uneasiness have not thought very long nor very hard about excellence in the United States.

TONING UP THE WHOLE SOCIETY

A conception that embraces many kinds of excellence at many levels is the only one that fully accords with the richly varied potentialities of mankind; it is the only one that will permit high morale throughout the society.

We have witnessed a revolution in society's attitude toward men and women of high ability and advanced training. Throughout the ages, human societies have been extravagantly wasteful of talent. But social and technological developments are forcing us to search for talent and to use it effectively. Among the historic changes of the twentieth century, this may in the long run prove to be one of the most profound.

—*Excellence*, 1961, p. 33

Living, Leading, and the American Dream

Our society cannot achieve greatness unless individuals at many levels of ability accept the need for high standards of performance and strive to achieve those standards within the limits possible for them. We want the highest conceivable excellence, of course, in the activities crucial to our effectiveness and creativity as a society, but that isn't enough. We must foster a conception of excellence that may be applied to every degree of ability and to every socially acceptable activity. A plane may crash because the designer was incompetent or because the mechanic responsible for maintenance was incompetent. The same is true of everything else in our society. We need excellent physicists and excellent construction workers, excellent legislators and excellent first-grade teachers. The tone and fiber of our society depend upon a pervasive, almost universal striving for good performance.

And we are not going to get that kind of striving, that kind of alert and proud attention to performance, unless we can instruct the whole society in a conception of excellence that leaves room for everybody who is willing to strive—a conception of excellence which says that whoever I am or whatever I am doing, provided that I am engaged in a socially acceptable activity, some kind of excellence is within my reach. As James B. Conant put it, "Each honest calling, each walk of life, has its own elite, its own aristocracy based upon excellence of performance."

We must learn to honor excellence in every socially accepted human performance, however humble the activity, and to scorn shoddiness, however exalted the activity. An excellent plumber is infinitely more admirable than an incompetent philosopher. The society that scorns excellence in plumbing because plumbing is a humble activity and tolerates shoddiness in philosophy because it is an exalted activity will have neither good plumbing nor good philosophy. Neither its pipes nor its theories will hold water.

—*Excellence,* 1961, p. 86

The Full Expression of Human Excellence

We cannot meet the challenges facing our society unless we can achieve and maintain a high level of morale and drive throughout the society. Men and women must have goals that in their own eyes merit effort and commitment, and they must believe that their efforts will win them self-respect and the respect of others.

It is important to bear in mind that we are talking about an approach to excellence and a conception of excellence that will bring a whole society to the peak of performance. The gifted individual absorbed in his own problems of creativity and workmanship may wish to set himself narrow and very severe standards of excellence. The critic concerned with a particular development in art, let us say, may wish to impose a specialized criterion of excellence. This is understandable. But we are concerned with a broader objective.

This broader objective is critically important, even for those who have set themselves far loftier (and narrower) personal standards of excellence. We cannot have islands of excellence in a sea of slovenly indifference to standards. In an era when the masses of people were mute and powerless it may have been possible for a tiny minority to maintain high standards regardless of their surroundings. But today the masses of people are neither mute nor powerless. As consumers, as voters, as the source of public opinion, they heavily influence levels of taste and performance. They can create a climate supremely inimical to standards of any sort.

I am not saying that we can expect everyone to be excellent. It would please me if this were possible: I am not one of those who believe that a goal is somehow unworthy if everyone can achieve it. But those who achieve excellence will be few at best. All too many lack the qualities of mind or spirit that would allow them to conceive excellence as a goal or to achieve it if they conceived it.

But many more can achieve it than now do. Many, many more can try to achieve it than now do. *And the society is bettered not only by those who achieve it but by those who are trying.*

The broad conception of excellence we have outlined must be built on two foundation stones—and both of them exist in our society.

- *A pluralistic approach to values.* American society has always leaned toward such pluralism. We need only be true to our deepest inclinations to honor the many facets and depth and dimensions of human experience and to seek the many kinds of excellence of which the human spirit is capable.

- *A universally honored philosophy of individual fulfillment.* We have such a philosophy, deeply embedded in our tradition.

The question of excellence is only one of the many problems facing a free society. But it is a problem that cuts across all the others. If a society holds conflicting views about excellence—or cannot rouse itself to the pursuit of excellence—the consequences will be felt in everything that it undertakes. The disease may not attack every organ, but the resulting debility will be felt in all parts of the system. Everything that it does and everything that it strives for will be affected.

12

Our Moral and Spiritual Lineage

In a world of tumultuous and frightening change, how do we face the future with courage? We cannot know what the future will bring, John W. Gardner tells us, but we can look back across the years, indeed the centuries, for examples of "men and women who continued stubbornly to seek justice and liberty and a world that honored the worth and dignity of each person." Their example, our moral and spiritual lineage, can give us strength today.

The most powerful moving forces in history are not societies—which are forever decaying—but highly motivated people and their ideas of what is worth living for and striving for.

Every year tens of millions of Americans come to the nation's capital to visit our national shrines. Day after day one sees them streaming through the Lincoln Memorial, the Washington Monument, the Capitol. But the spirit of the nation does not reside in the physical structures. It is in the minds of the citizens who come to look at the structures. That is where a vital society begins; if it ends, that is where it ends. If they stop believing, if they lose faith, if they stop caring, the monuments will be meaningless piles of stone, and the nation will be as lifeless as the stones. There will still be the land and a lot of people milling around, but the venture that began with the Declaration of Independence, the venture familiarly known as America, will be dead.

> The worst of our problems is not that the old vision is fading. Old visions are always fading. The question is whether we have lost the capacity to generate a new vision—or the capacity to tolerate visions.
>
> —*In Common Cause*, 1972, p. 101

It need not happen. But it could. The task of the moment is to re-create a motivated society. If we fail in that, forget the rest. When a society disintegrates, you may be sure that its animating ideas and ideals died first in the minds of men and women.

THE UNKNOWABLE FUTURE

A Chinese proverb says, "To prophesy is extremely difficult—especially with respect to the future." A nineteenth-century horse breeder foresaw the day when transportation would be wholly revolutionized by the breeding of a horse that could run at a pace of fifty miles an hour indefinitely. The Wright brothers thought that invention of the airplane would bring an end to all wars, because under observation from the air no military force could maneuver secretly.

If it's hard to know the shape of things to come, it's virtually impossible to design social arrangements for that unknown future. It is tempting to imagine that we can draw neat blueprints of a society that will serve future generations, but we cannot. This truth is ignored to the point of comedy by many of the earnest voices that tell us how to reconstruct our society. There's a chronic shortage of people who can solve our problems here and now, but never a shortage of people who will tell us how to design our society for an unpredictable future. They woefully underestimate the imponderables of social change, especially now, when its swift flow threatens the continuities of human experience in ways we can hardly imagine.

We cannot design today the institutions for a future we cannot foretell. The best we can do is to foster the kinds of men and women who can cope with the future as it unfolds, who are capable of facing new realities as they emerge without forgetting the continuities in our tradition and our longer-term aspirations as a free people. If we are to create a society for the transitions ahead that is worthy of our heritage of freedom, our surest resource will be men and women of courage and conviction who carry within themselves a sense of what is important for the human future, a sense of what makes societies vital and humane.

A SYSTEM THAT EVOLVES

With the old ways losing their hold and new ways yet to be shaped, it will be useful to remember that the time-honored customs and arrangements of a society—its institutions—have never been the solid foundation that they are widely assumed to be. They are creations of the human mind, forever changing.

We might find contemporary changes less disturbing if we reflected on the profound transformations that have already occurred in our own history. When the British colonized North America, they assumed that they could transport their institutions and attitudes to these shores more or less intact, but before the seventeenth century ended, the North American colonists had created a strikingly new way of life. They had developed attitudes and social arrangements that made the Revolution almost inevitable.

In earlier times one generation might create value patterns that several following generations would live by unquestioningly. It was as though one generation built the houses, and succeeding generations lived in them, forgetting their own building skills in the process. Today we are more like people in a land of recurring earthquakes and tornadoes, where each generation must keep its building skills fresh and in fact rebuild almost continuously.

—*Self-Renewal* (Rev. ed.), 1981, p. xiv

That was the first America. It wasn't born in 1776; that's when it was old enough to leave home. It underwent marked changes, particularly with the emergence of Jacksonian democracy, but from beginning to end it was rural, essentially preindustrial, overwhelmingly Protestant, and relatively insulated from the rest of the world.

Then in the mid-nineteenth century the first America slowly disappeared; and a very different society took shape as the powerful stirrings of industrialism began their transforming work. The second America was increasingly urban, secular, industrial, heavily salted with immigrants, pursuing ardently the revolutions in communication and transportation, and immensely exhilarated by its own growth. The third America, which came in with Franklin D. Roosevelt, was acutely conscious of social issues and committed to use the power of the federal government to resolve those issues. It was also internationalist and—ultimately—enormously preoccupied with the arts of war. (I have sketched the three Americas in grossly oversimplified terms, but the reader will recognize the underlying reality of profound social change.)

Now we are undergoing another transition. We cannot know what the next America will be like, but no one who reflects on the profound alterations—economic, political, and social—that accompanied past transitions can doubt that "the American system"—so often piously regarded as immutable—is in fact changing continuously, all the while retaining powerful continuities of character and spirit.

It isn't enough to tell people that they must be equal to the challenges the future will bring. The contemporary mind asks, "Why? What makes it worthwhile? What can I believe? What can I admire and take sustenance from?"

The question isn't easily answered. Around the individual today swirls a bewildering jumble of faiths, heresies, and unbelief. It's hard for any thoughtful person to observe, in Cardinal Newman's words, "the defeat of good, the success of evil . . . the pervading idolatries, the corruptions" and still find ground for moral striving.

It isn't only the modern mind that has had difficulty with such questions. More than two thousand years ago, Ecclesiastes, who had a boundless capacity to be disappointed by the world, was particularly troubled that one cannot expect just rewards in this life. It concerned him that the wise man fares no better than the fool, the righteous no better than the wicked. The race is not to the swift: "Time and chance happeneth to them all."

It is true that there is no assurance of reward for effort or wisdom or talent or virtue, at least not in the terms that the world commonly reckons rewards—money, status, acclaim, pleasure, or power. Sensible people grasp that reality fairly early.

So why bother to meet any standards of behavior? Why strive to diminish human suffering? Why combat injustice? For some the answer may lie in being true to their religious convictions; for others, in expressing their allegiance to a moral order (however they may conceive it); for still others, simply in trying to be true to what humans can be at their best.

"Trying to be true to what humans can be at their best." The words are deceptively simple, but the idea has great power. Humans have shown themselves capable of degradation as well as nobility, of cruelty as well as kindness, of greed as well as generosity. To pretend that the darker side of human nature dissolves under the cleansing rays of idealism is to delude oneself. Even in those moments of human history when corruption and degradation seemed wholly triumphant, there were some men and women who continued stubbornly to seek justice and liberty and a world that honored the worth and dignity of each person; there were those who strove for excellence; there were those who tried to create a more humane environment for those around them. Some left their names in the history books, others were well known in their time and place but are unknown to us; and some were perhaps never heard of beyond their neighborhood. You have known such people. Some have bettered the lives of millions, others may have helped only a few among their immediate family and friends. It doesn't matter.

An enduring basis for moral commitment is to affirm our allegiance to those men and women, to associate ourselves with the human spirit striving for the best. To remind ourselves that they existed is a message of solidarity for every seriously striving person.

Most of the ingredients of a vision for this country have been with us for a long time. As the poet wrote, "The light we sought is shining still." That we have failed and fumbled in some of our attempts to achieve our ideals is obvious. But the great ideas still beckon—freedom, equality, justice, the release of human possibilities.

—Speech at the Kellogg-Kauffman Aspen Conference, Aspen, Colorado, 1993

There is no evidence that humans can perfect themselves or their societies. But their impulse to try accounts for the best moments in humankind's stormy history. People of various religious and philosophical views explain the impulse in varying terminology, but few deny that it exists. The impulse may be layered over, ignored, or smothered by worldliness and cynicism, but it is there—and, in some people, inextinguishable. We draw our spiritual strength from just those people, even though most of them are unknown to us. They are the bearers of the spirit, the lifeline of the race, stretching back through the centuries.

CONTINUITIES OF THE SPIRIT

All of us celebrate our values in our behavior. The way we act and conduct our lives says something to others—perhaps something reprehensible, perhaps something encouraging. We are teaching by example—bad lessons or good. Each of us is saying—in our behavior—"This is one thing of which humankind is capable." We are allying ourselves with those who have exalted humankind or with those who have degraded it. All those who set standards for themselves, rear their children responsibly, strengthen the bonds of community, do their work creditably and accept individual responsibility are building the common future. It is the universal ministry.

This is a heartening truth for those people who wish to assist in the regeneration of values but can't imagine how they can possibly influence this huge and complex society. They are not as powerless as they believe. No one can measure the contagion of ideas, values, and aspirations as expressed in the lives and acts of individual men and women. That contagion produces continuities in social behavior that are not readily discernible. We are familiar with the continuities evident in the influence of great teachers, prophets, and philosophers, but we have given little thought to the moral and spiritual lineage of everyday human interaction. We couldn't possibly name the many people who have influenced us, sometimes through a single exemplary act. As they influenced us, others influenced them. Those living today will influence others. The web of influence reaches back through the generations, stretching over centuries a skein of incomparable delicacy and strength. That moral and spiritual lineage, often preserved at great cost, is an antidote to the cynicism so often generated by the contemporary inflated self, which seeks all meaning in its own aches and itches.

PART FOUR

Leading and Managing

13

The Nature of Leadership

Leadership was a central theme for John W. Gardner. In World War II he observed it in time of crisis; as a foundation officer, he looked for it in the projects he supported; as a cabinet officer, managing a gigantic federal bureaucracy, he had to identify leadership talent both inside and outside to move his agenda forward; and as the founder of several new organizations, he realized that effective leadership was a key to success. After twenty-five years of writing on various aspects of the subject, he took five years to explore the literature, meet with scholars, and visit study centers. He wrote twelve individual essays on leadership, which were published by INDEPENDENT SECTOR, and then revised them for his book *On Leadership* (1990). This selection, from the first chapter of that book, begins his discussion with an analysis of just what leadership is, and what it is not.

Leadership is a word that has risen above normal workaday usage as a conveyor of meaning. There seems to be a feeling that if we invoke it often enough with sufficient ardor we can ease our sense of having lost our way, our sense of things unaccomplished, of duties unfulfilled.

All of that simply clouds our thinking. The aura with which we tend to surround the words *leader* and *leadership* makes it hard to think clearly. Good sense calls for demystification.

Leadership is the process of persuasion or example by which an individual (or leadership team) induces a group to pursue objectives held by the leader or shared by the leader and his or her followers.

In any established group, individuals fill different roles, and one of the roles is that of leader. Leaders cannot be thought of apart from the historic context in which they arise, the setting in which they function (for example, elective political office), and the system over which they preside (such as a particular city or state). They are integral parts of the system, subject to the forces that affect the system. They perform (or cause to be performed) certain tasks or functions that are essential if the group is to accomplish its purposes.

All that we know about the interaction between leaders and constituents or followers tells us that communication and influence flow in both directions; and in that two-way communication, nonrational, nonverbal, and unconscious elements play their part. In the process leaders shape and are shaped. This is true even in systems that appear to be led in quite autocratic fashion. In a state governed by coercion, followers cannot prevent the leader from violating their customs and beliefs, but they have many ways of making it more costly to violate than to honor their norms, and leaders usually make substantial accommodations. If Julius Caesar had been willing to live more flexibly with the give-and-take he might not have been slain in the Senate. Machiavelli, the ultimate realist, advised his prince, "You will always need the favor of the inhabitants. It is necessary for a prince to possess the friendship of the people."[1]

The connotations of the word *follower* suggest too much passivity and dependence to make it a fit term for all who are at the other end of the dialogue with leaders. I don't intend to discard it, but I also make frequent use of the word *constituent*. It is awkward in some contexts, but often it does fuller justice to the two-way interchange.

Elements of physical coercion are involved in some kinds of leadership, and of course there is psychological coercion, however mild and subtle, including peer pressure, in all social action. But in our culture, popular understanding of the leadership process distinguishes it from coercion—and places those forms involving the least coercion higher on the scale of leadership.

I write particularly of leadership in this country today. Examples are drawn from other cultures and many of the generalizations are relevant for all times and places, but the focus is here and now. The points empha-

Living, Leading, and the American Dream

sized might be different were I writing fifty years ago or fifty years hence, or writing of Bulgaria or Tibet.

DISTINCTIONS

We must not confuse leadership with status. Even in large corporations and government agencies, the top-ranking person may simply be bureaucrat number one. We have all occasionally encountered top persons who couldn't lead a squad of seven-year-olds to the ice cream counter.

It does not follow that status is irrelevant to leadership. Most positions of high status carry with them symbolic values and traditions that enhance the possibility of leadership. People expect governors and corporation presidents to lead, which heightens the possibility that they will. But the selection process for positions of high status does not make that a sure outcome.

Similarly, we must not confuse leadership with power. Leaders always have some measure of power, rooted in their capacity to persuade, but many people with power are without leadership gifts. Their power derives from money, or from the capacity to inflict harm, or from control of some piece of institutional machinery, or from access to the media. A military dictator has power. The thug who sticks a gun in your ribs has power. Leadership is something else.

To say a leader is preoccupied with power is like saying that a tennis player is preoccupied with making shots an opponent cannot return. Of course leaders are preoccupied with power! The significant questions are: What means do they use to gain it? How do they exercise it? To what ends do they exercise it?

—*On Leadership*, 1990, p. 57

Finally, we must not confuse leadership with official authority, which is simply legitimized power. Meter maids have it; the person who audits your tax returns has it.

Confusion between leadership and official authority has a deadly effect on large organizations. Corporations and government agencies everywhere have executives who imagine that their place on the organization chart has given them a body of followers. And of course it has not. They have been given subordinates. Whether the subordinates become followers depends on whether the executives act like leaders.

Is it appropriate to apply to leaders the word *elite?* The word was once applied to families of exalted social status. Then sociologists adopted the word to describe any group of high status, whether hereditary or earned; thus, in addition to the elites of old families and old money, there are elites of performance and profession.

Some social critics today use the word with consistent negative overtones. They believe that elite status is incompatible with an equalitarian philosophy. But in any society—no matter how democratic, no matter how equalitarian—there are elites in the sociologist's sense: intellectual, athletic, artistic, political, and others. The marks of an open society are that elite status is generally earned, and that those who have earned it do not use their status to violate democratic norms. In our society, leaders are among the many "performance elites."

Leaders and Managers

The word *manager* usually indicates that the individual so labeled holds a directive post in an organization, presiding over the processes by which the organization functions, allocating resources prudently, and making the best possible use of people.

Many writers on leadership take considerable pains to distinguish between leaders and managers. In the process leaders generally end up looking like a cross between Napoleon and the Pied Piper, and managers like unimaginative clods. This troubles me. I once heard it said of a man, "He's an utterly first-class manager but there isn't a trace of the leader in him." I am still looking for that man, and I am beginning to believe that he does not exist. Every time I encounter utterly first-class managers they turn out to have quite a lot of the leader in them.

Even the most visionary leader is faced on occasion with decisions that every manager faces: when to take a short-term loss to achieve a long-term gain, how to allocate scarce resources, whom to trust with a delicate assignment. So even though it has become conventional to contrast leaders and managers, I am inclined to use slightly different categories, lumping leaders and leader-managers into one category and placing in the other category those numerous managers whom one would not normally describe as leaders. Leaders and leader-managers distinguish themselves from the general run of managers in at least six respects:

- They think longer term—beyond the day's crises, beyond the quarterly report, beyond the horizon.

- In thinking about the unit they are heading, they grasp its relationship to larger realities—the larger organization of which they are a part, conditions external to the organization, global trends.

- They reach and influence constituents beyond their jurisdictions, beyond boundaries. Thomas Jefferson influenced people all over Europe. Gandhi influenced people all over the world. In an organization, leaders extend their reach across bureaucratic boundaries—often a distinct advantage in a world too complex and tumultuous to be handled through channels. Leaders' capacity to rise above jurisdictions may enable them to bind together the fragmented constituencies that must work together to solve a problem.

- They put heavy emphasis on the intangibles of vision, values, and motivation and understand intuitively the nonrational and unconscious elements in leader-constituent interaction.

- They have the political skill to cope with the conflicting requirements of multiple constituencies.

- They think in terms of renewal. The routine manager tends to accept organizational structure and process as it exists. The leader or leader-manager seeks the revisions of process and structure required by ever-changing reality.

The manager is more tightly linked to an organization than is the leader. Indeed, the leader may have no organization at all. Florence Nightingale, after leaving the Crimea, exercised extraordinary leadership in health care for decades with no organization under her command. Gandhi was a leader before he had an organization. Some of our most memorable leaders have headed movements so amorphous that *management* would be an inappropriate word.

The Many Kinds of Leaders

One hears and reads a surprising number of sentences that describe leaders in general as having such-and-such attributes and behaving in such-and-such a fashion—as though one could distill out of the spectacular diversity of leaders an idealized picture of The Leader.

Leaders come in many forms, with many styles and diverse qualities. There are quiet leaders and leaders one can hear in the next county. Some find their strength in eloquence, some in judgment, some in courage. I had a friend who was a superior leader in outdoor activities and sports but quite incapable of leading in a bureaucratic setting.

The diversity is almost without limit: Churchill, the splendidly eloquent old warrior; Gandhi, the visionary and the shrewd mobilizer of his people; Lenin, the coldly purposeful revolutionary. Consider just the limited category of military leadership. George Marshall was a self-effacing, low-keyed man with superb judgment and a limitless capacity to inspire trust. MacArthur was a brilliant strategist, a farsighted administrator, and flamboyant to his fingertips. (Eisenhower, who had served under MacArthur, once said, "I studied dramatics under a master.") Eisenhower in his wartime assignment was an outstanding leader-administrator and coalition builder. General Patton was a slashing, intense combat commander. Field Marshal Montgomery was a gifted, temperamental leader of whom Churchill said, "In defeat, indomitable; in victory, insufferable." All were great leaders—but extraordinarily diverse in personal attributes.

The fact that there are many kinds of leaders has implications for leadership education. Most of those seeking to develop young potential leaders have in mind one ideal model that is inevitably constricting. We should give

118

young people a sense of the many kinds of leaders and styles of leadership, and encourage them to move toward those models that are right for them.

Leaders and History

All too often when we think of our historic leaders, we eliminate all the contradictions that make individuals distinctive. And we further violate reality by lifting them out of their historical contexts. No wonder we are left with pasteboard portraits. As first steps toward a mature view of leaders we must accept complexity and context.

Thomas Jefferson was first of all a gifted and many-sided human, an enigmatic man who loved—among other things—abstract ideas, agriculture, architecture and statecraft. He was a man of natural aloofness who lived most of his life in public; a man of action with a gift for words and a bent for research; an idealist who proved himself a shrewd, even wily, operator on the political scene. Different sides of his nature came into play in different situations.

Place him now in the context of the exhilarating events and themes of his time: a new nation coming into being, with a new consciousness; the brilliant rays of the Enlightenment reaching into every phase of life; the inner contradictions of American society (for example, slavery) already rumbling beneath the surface.

Finally, add the overpowering impulse of succeeding generations to serve their own needs by mythologizing, idolizing or debunking him. It turns out to be an intricately textured story—and not one that diminishes Jefferson.

It was once believed that if leadership traits were truly present in an individual, they would manifest themselves almost without regard to the situation in which the person was functioning. No one believes that any more. Acts of leadership take place in an unimaginable variety of settings, and the setting does much to determine the kinds of leaders that emerge and how they play their roles.

We cannot avoid the bewhiskered question, "Does the leader make history or does the historical moment make the leader?" It sounds like a seminar question but it is of interest to most leaders sooner or later. Corporate chief executive officers fighting a deteriorating trend in an industry feel like people trying to run up the down escalator. Looking across town at less able leaders riding an upward trend in another industry, they are ripe for the theory that history makes the leader.

Thomas Carlyle placed excessive emphasis on the great person, as did Sidney Hook ("all factors in history, save great men, are inconsequential").[2] Karl Marx, Georg Hegel, and Herbert Spencer placed excessive emphasis on historical forces. For Marx, economic forces shaped history; for Spencer, societies had their evolutionary course just as species did, and the leader was a product of the process; for Hegel, leaders were a part of the dialectic of history and could not help what they did.

The balanced view, of course, is that historical forces create the circumstances in which leaders emerge, but the characteristics of the particular leader in turn have their impact on history.

It is not possible to understand Queen Isabella without understanding fifteenth-century Europe (when she was born, Spain as we know it did not exist), or without understanding the impact of the Reformation on the Catholic world and the gnawing fear stirred by the Muslim conquests. But many monarchs flourished on the Iberian Peninsula in that historical context; only Isabella left an indelible mark. Similarly, by the time Martin Luther emerged, the seeds of the Reformation had already sprouted in many places, but no one would argue that the passionate, charismatic priest who nailed his ninety-five theses to the church door was a puppet of history. Historical forces set the stage for him, but once there, he was himself a historical force.

Churchill is an even more interesting case because he tried out for leadership many times before history was ready for him. After Dunkirk, England needed a leader who could rally the British people to heroic exertions in an uncompromising war, and the eloquent, combative Churchill delivered one of the great performances of the century. Subsequently the clock of history ticked on and—with the war over—the voters dropped him unceremoniously. When a friend told him it was a blessing in disguise, he growled, "If it is, the disguise is perfect."

Forces of history determined his rise and fall, but in his time on the world stage he left a uniquely Churchillian mark on the course of events.

SETTINGS

The historical moment is the broadest context affecting the emergence and functioning of leaders; but immensely diverse settings of a more modest nature clearly affect leadership.

The makeup of the group to be led is, of course, a crucial feature of the context. According to research findings, the approach to leadership or style of leadership that will be effective depends on, among other things, the age level of the individuals to be led; their educational background and competence; the size, homogeneity and cohesiveness of the group; its motivation and morale; and its rate of turnover.

> Despite the lavish media attention to high-level leaders, we are not wholly dependent on leadership at the top. We are dependent on leaders at many levels and in all segments of our society—business, government, organized labor, agriculture, the professions, the minority communities, the arts, the universities, social agencies. They are city councilmen and school superintendents, factory managers and editors, heads of local unions and heads of social agencies, lawyers and health commissioners.
>
> If it weren't for this wide dispersal of leadership, our kind of society couldn't function. Excessive dependence on central definition and rule-making produces standardized solutions to be applied uniformly throughout the system. But the world "out there," the world to be coped with, isn't standardized. It is diverse, localized, and surprising.
>
> —*Excellence* (Rev. ed.), 1984, p. 135

Other relevant contextual features are too numerous and diverse to list. Leading a corporation is one thing, leading a street gang is something else. Thomas Cronin has pointed out that it may take one kind of leadership to start a new enterprise and quite another kind to keep it going through its various phases.[3] Religious bodies, political parties, government agencies, the academic world—all offer distinctive contexts for leadership.

JUDGMENTS OF LEADERS

In curious ways, people tend to aggrandize the role of leaders. They tend to exaggerate the capacity of leaders to influence events. Jeffrey Pfeffer says that people want to achieve a feeling of control over their environment, and that this inclines them to attribute the outcomes of group performance to leaders rather than to context.[4] If we were to face the fact—so the argument goes—that outcomes are the result of a complex set of interactions among group members plus environmental and historical forces, we would feel helpless. By attributing outcomes to an identifiable leader we feel, rightly or not, more in control. There is at least a chance that one can fire the leader; one cannot "fire" historical forces.

Leaders act in the stream of history. As they labor to bring about a result, multiple forces beyond their control, even beyond their knowledge, are moving to hasten or hinder the result. So there is rarely a demonstrable causal link between a leader's specific decisions and consequent events. Consequences are not a reliable measure of leadership. Franklin Roosevelt's efforts to bolster the economy in the middle to late 1930s were powerfully aided by a force that did not originate with his economic brain trust—the winds of war. Leaders of a farm workers' union fighting for better wages may find their efforts set at naught by a crop failure.

Frank Lloyd Wright said, "A doctor can bury his mistakes. An architect can only advise his client to plant vines." Unlike either doctor or architect, leaders suffer from the mistakes of predecessors and leave some of their own misjudgments as time bombs for successors.

Many of the changes sought by leaders take time: lots of years, long public debate, slow shifts in attitude. In their lifetimes, leaders may see little result from heroic efforts yet may be setting the stage for victories that will come after them. Reflect on the long, slow unfolding of the battles for racial equality or for women's rights. Leaders who did vitally important early work died without knowing what they had wrought.

Leaders may appear to have succeeded (or failed) only to have historians a generation later reverse the verdict. The "verdict of history" has a wonderfully magisterial sound, but in reality it is subject to endless appeals to

Living, Leading, and the American Dream

later generations of historians—with no court of last resort to render a final judgment.

In the real world, the judgments one makes of a leader must be multidimensional, taking into consideration great strengths, streaks of mediocrity, and perhaps great flaws. If the great strengths correspond to the needs of a critical moment in history, the flaws are forgiven and simply provide texture to the biographies. Each leader has his or her own unique pattern of attributes, sometimes conflicting in curious ways. Ronald Reagan was notably passive with respect to many important issues, but vigorously tenacious on other issues.

Leaders change over the course of their active careers as do other human beings. In looking back, it is natural for us to freeze them in that moment when they served history's needs most spectacularly, but leaders evolve. The passionately antislavery Lincoln of the Douglas debates was not the see-both-sides Lincoln of fifteen years earlier. The "national unity" Churchill of 1942 was not the fiercely partisan, adversarial Churchill of the 1930s.

DEVOLVING INITIATIVE AND RESPONSIBILITY

I have already commented on our dispersed leadership and on its importance to the vitality of a large, intricately organized system. Our most forward-looking business concerns are working in quite imaginative ways to devolve initiative downward and outward through their organizations to develop their lower levels of leadership. There is no comparable movement in government agencies. But in the nation as a whole, dispersed leadership is a reality.

The leaders of the Soviet Union did not launch the reforms of 1987 because they had developed a sudden taste for grassroots democracy. They launched them because their system was grinding to a halt. Leader-managers at the lower levels and at the periphery of the system had neither the motivation nor the authority to solve problems that they understood better than the Moscow bureaucrats.

We have only half learned the lesson ourselves. In many of our large corporate, governmental, and nonprofit organizations we still make it all too difficult for potential leaders down the line to exercise initiative. We are still in the process of discovering how much vitality and motivation are buried at those levels awaiting release.

> Leaders must understand that for most men and women the driving energies are latent. Some individuals are unaware of their potentialities, some are sleepwalking through the routines of life, some have succumbed to a sense of defeat. What one sees on the surface can be discouraging. What leaders have to remember is that somewhere under that somnolent surface are the creatures that build civilizations, the dreamers of dreams, the risk-takers.
>
> —Speech at the White House Fellows Reunion, Washington, D.C., 1991

To emphasize the need for dispersed leadership does not deny the need for highly qualified top leadership. But our high-level leaders will be more effective in every way if the systems over which they preside are made vital by dispersed leadership. As I argued in *Excellence,* we must demand high performance at every level of society.[5]

INSTITUTIONALIZING LEADERSHIP

To exercise leadership today, leaders must institutionalize their leadership. The issues are too technical and the pace of change too swift to expect that a leader, no matter how gifted, will be able to solve personally the major problems facing the system over which he or she presides. So we design an institutional system—a government agency, a corporation—to solve the problems, and then we select a leader who has the capacity to preside over and strengthen the system. Some leaders may be quite gifted in solving problems personally, but if they fail to institutionalize the process, their departure leaves the system crippled. They must create or strengthen systems that will survive them.

The institutional arrangements generally include a leadership team. Often when I use the word *leader*, I am in fact referring to the leadership team. No individual has all the skills—and certainly not the time—to carry out all the complex tasks of contemporary leadership. And the team must be chosen for excellence in performance. Loyalty and being on the boss's wavelength are necessary but not sufficient qualifications. I emphasize the point because more than one recent president of the United States had aides who possessed no other qualifications.

The Tasks of Leadership

"The first task of a leader is to keep hope alive." Important additional tasks include setting goals, affirming values, motivating constituents, managing and building organizations, defusing conflict, explaining and teaching, serving as a symbol and representative of the group, and renewing. John W. Gardner explored the dimensions of each of these.

Examination of the tasks performed by leaders takes us to the heart of some of the most interesting questions concerning leadership. It also helps to distinguish among the many kinds of leaders. Leaders differ strikingly in how well they perform various functions.

The following tasks seem to me to be the most significant functions of leadership, but I encourage readers to add to the list or to describe the tasks in other ways. Leadership activities implicit in all of the tasks (such as communicating or relating effectively with people) are not dealt with separately.

ENVISIONING GOALS

The two tasks at the heart of the popular notion of leadership are goal setting and motivating. As a high school senior put it, "Leaders point us in the right direction and tell us to get moving." Although we take a more complicated view of the tasks of leadership, it is appropriate that we begin with the envisioning of goals. Albert Einstein said, "Perfection of means and confusion of ends seems to characterize our age."

Leaders perform the function of goal setting in diverse ways. Some assert a vision of what the group (organization, community, nation) can be at its best. Others point us toward solutions to our problems. Still others, presiding over internally divided groups, are able to define overarching goals that unify constituencies and focus energies. In today's complex world, the setting of goals may have to be preceded by extensive research and problem solving.

Obviously, a constituency is not a blank slate for the leader to write on. Any collection of people sufficiently related to be called a community has many shared goals, some explicit, some unexpressed (perhaps even unconscious), as tangible as better prices for their crops, as intangible as a better future for their children. In a democracy, the leader takes such shared goals into account.

The relative roles of leaders and followers in determining goals vary from group to group. The teacher of first-grade children and the sergeant training recruits do not do extensive consulting as to goals; congressional candidates do a great deal. In the case of many leaders, goals are handed to them by higher authority. The factory manager and the combat commander may be superb leaders, but many of their goals are set at higher levels.

In short, goals emerge from many sources. The culture itself specifies certain goals; constituents have their concerns; higher authority makes its wishes known. Out of the welter, leaders take some goals as given, and making their own contribution, select and formulate a set of objectives. It may sound as though leaders have only marginal freedom, but in fact there is usually considerable opportunity, even for lower-level leaders, to put their personal emphasis and interpretation on the setting of goals.

There is inevitable tension between long- and short-term goals. On one hand, constituents are not entirely comfortable with the jerkiness of short-term goal seeking, and they value the sense of stability that comes with a vision of far horizons. On the other hand, long-term goals may require them to defer immediate gratification on at least some fronts. Leaders often fear that when citizens enter the voting booth, they will remember the deferral of gratification more vividly than they remember the reason for it.

Before the Civil War, Elizabeth Cady Stanton saw virtually the whole agenda for women's rights as it was to emerge over the succeeding century.

Many of her contemporaries in the movement were not at all prepared for such an inclusive vision and urged her to play it down.

Another visionary far ahead of his time was the South American liberator Simón Bolívar. He launched his fight in that part of Gran Colombia which is now Venezuela, but in his mind was a vision not only of independence for all of Spain's possessions in the New World but also a peaceful alliance of the new states in some form of league or confederation. Although he was tragically ahead of his time, the dream never died and has influenced generations of Latin American leaders striving toward unity.

AFFIRMING VALUES

A great civilization is a drama lived in the minds of a people. It is a shared vision; it is shared norms, expectations, and purposes. When one thinks of the world's great civilizations the most vivid images that crowd in on us are apt to be of the physical monuments left behind—the pyramids, the Parthenon, the Mayan temples. But in truth, all the physical splendor was the merest by-product. The civilizations themselves, from beginning to end, existed in the minds of men and women.

If we look at ordinary human communities, we see the same reality: A community lives in the minds of its members—in shared assumptions, beliefs, customs, ideas that give meaning, ideas that motivate. And among the ideas are norms or values. In any healthy, reasonably coherent community, people come to have shared views concerning right and wrong, better and worse—in personal conduct, in governing, in art, whatever. They define for their time and place what things are legal or illegal, virtuous or vicious, good taste or bad. They have little or no impulse to be neutral about such matters. Every society is, as Philip Rieff puts it, "a system of moralizing demands."[1]

Values are embodied in the society's religious beliefs and its secular philosophy. Over the past century, many intellectuals have looked down on the celebration of our values as an unsophisticated and often hypocritical activity. But every healthy society celebrates its values. They are expressed in art, in song, in ritual. They are stated explicitly in historical documents, in ceremonial speeches, in textbooks. They are reflected in stories told around the campfire, in the legends kept alive by old folks, in the fables told to children.

In a pluralistic community there are, within the broad consensus that enables the community to function, many and vigorous conflicts over specific values.

THE REGENERATION OF VALUES

One of the milder pleasures of maturity is bemoaning the decay of values once strongly held. *Values always decay over time. Societies that keep their values alive do so not by escaping the processes of decay but by powerful processes of regeneration.* There must be perpetual rebuilding. Each generation must rediscover the living elements in its own tradition and adapt them to present realities. To assist in that rediscovery is one of the tasks of leadership.

The leaders whom we admire the most help to revitalize our shared beliefs and values. They have always spent a portion of their time teaching the value framework.

Sometimes the leader's affirmation of values challenges entrenched hypocrisy or conflicts with the values held by a segment of the constituency. Elizabeth Cady Stanton, speaking for now-accepted values, was regarded as a thoroughgoing radical in her day.[2] Jesus not only comforted the afflicted but afflicted the comfortable.

MOTIVATING

Leaders do not create motivation out of thin air. They unlock or channel existing motives. Any group has a great tangle of motives. Effective leaders tap those that serve the purposes of collective action in pursuit of shared goals. They accomplish the alignment of individual and group goals. They deal with the circumstances that often lead group members to withhold their best efforts. They call for the kind of effort and restraint, drive and discipline that make for great performance. They create a climate in which there is pride in making significant contributions to shared goals.

> The first and last task of a leader is to keep hope alive—the hope that we can finally find our way through to a better world—despite the day's bitter discouragement, despite the perplexities of social action, despite our own shallowness and wavering resolve.
>
> —*No Easy Victories*, 1968, p. 134

Note that in the tasks of leadership, the transactions between leaders and constituents go beyond the rational level to the nonrational and unconscious levels of human functioning. Young potential leaders who have been schooled to believe that all elements of a problem are rational and technical, reducible to words and numbers, are ill-equipped to move into an area where intuition and empathy are powerful aids to problem solving.

MANAGING

Most managers exhibit some leadership skills, and most leaders on occasion find themselves managing. Leadership and management are not the same thing, but they overlap. It makes sense to include managing in the list of tasks leaders perform.

In the paragraphs that follow I focus on those aspects of leadership that one might describe as managing without slipping into a conventional description of managing as such. And I try to find terminology and phrasing broad enough to cover the diverse contexts in which leadership occurs in corporations, unions, municipalities, political movements, and the like.

Planning and Priority Setting

Assuming that broad goals have been set, someone has to plan, fix priorities, choose means, and formulate policy. These are functions often performed by leaders. When Lyndon B. Johnson said, early in his presidency, that education was the nation's number one priority, he galvanized the nation's educational leaders and released constructive energies far beyond any governmental action that had yet been taken. It was a major factor in leading me to accept a post in his Cabinet.

Organizing and Institution Building

We have all seen leaders enjoy their brilliant moment and then disappear without a trace because they had no gift for building their purposes into institutions. In the ranks of leaders, Alfred Sloan was at the other extreme. Though he sold a lot of automobiles, he was not primarily a salesman; he was an institution builder. His understanding of organization was intuitive and profound.

Someone has to design the structures and processes through which substantial endeavors get accomplished over time. Ideally, leaders should not regard themselves as indispensable but should enable the group to carry on. Institutions are a means to that end. Jean Monnet said, "Nothing is possible without individuals; nothing is lasting without institutions."[3]

Keeping the System Functioning

Presiding over the arrangements through which individual energies are coordinated to achieve shared goals sounds like a quintessential management task. But it is clear that most leaders find themselves occasionally performing one or another of the essential chores: mobilizing and allocating resources; staffing and ensuring the continuing vitality of the team; creating and maintaining appropriate procedures; directing, delegating and coordinating; providing a system of incentives; reporting, evaluating and holding accountable.

Agenda Setting and Decision Making

The goals may be clear and the organization well set up and smoothly operating, but there remain agenda-setting and decision-making functions that must be dealt with. The announcement of goals without a proposed program for meeting them is a familiar enough political phenomenon—but not one that builds credibility. There are leaders who can motivate and inspire but who cannot visualize a path to the goal in practical, feasible steps. Leaders who lack that skill must bring onto their team people who have it.

One of the purest examples of the leader as agenda setter was Florence Nightingale.[4] Her public image was and is that of the lady of mercy, but under her gentle manner, she was a rugged spirit, a fighter, a tough-minded system changer. She never made public appearances or speeches, and except for her two years in the Crimea, held no public position. Her strength was that she was a formidable authority on the evils to be remedied, she knew what to do about them, and she used public opinion to goad top officials to adopt her agenda.

Exercising Political Judgment

In our pluralistic society, persons directing substantial enterprises find that they are presiding over many constituencies within their organizations and contending with many outside. Each has its needs and claims. One of the tasks of the leader-manager is to make the political judgments necessary to prevent secondary conflicts of purpose from blocking progress toward primary goals. Sometimes the literature on administration and management treats politics as an alien and disruptive force. But Aaron Wildavsky, in his brilliant book, *The Nursing Father: Moses as a Political Leader,* makes the point that leaders are inevitably political.[5]

ACHIEVING WORKABLE UNITY

A pluralistic society is, by definition, one that accepts many different elements, each with its own purposes. Collisions are inevitable and often healthy—as in commercial competition, in civil suits, and in efforts to redress grievances through the political process. Conflict is necessary in the case of oppressed groups that must fight for the justice that is due them. All our elective officials know the intense conflict of the political campaign. Indeed, one could argue that willingness to engage in battle when necessary is a sine qua non of leadership.

But most leaders most of the time are striving to diminish conflict rather than increase it. Some measure of cohesion and mutual tolerance is an absolute requirement of social functioning.

Sometimes the problem is not outright conflict but an unwillingness to cooperate. One of the gravest problems George Washington faced as a general was that the former colonies, though they had no doubt they were all on the same side, were not always sure they wanted to cooperate. As late as 1818, John Randolph declared, "When I speak of my country, I mean the Commonwealth of Virginia."[6]

The unifying function of leaders is well illustrated in the actions of George Bush after winning the presidential election of 1988. He promptly met with his defeated opponent, Michael Dukakis; with his chief rival for the nomination, Senator Robert Dole; and with Jesse Jackson and Coretta Scott King, both of whom had opposed his election. He asked Jack Kemp, another of his rivals for the nomination, to be Secretary of Housing and Urban Development, and Senator Dole's wife, Elizabeth Hanford Dole, to be Secretary of Labor.

Leaders in this country today must cope with the fragmentation of the society into groups that have great difficulty in understanding one another or agreeing on common goals. It is a fragmentation rooted in the pluralism of our society, in the obsessive specialization of modern life, and in the skill with which groups organize to advance their concerns.

Under the circumstances, all our leaders must spend part of their time dealing with polarization and building community. There is a false notion that this is a more bland, less rigorous task than leadership of one of the combative segments. In fact, the leader willing to combat polarization is the braver person, and is generally under fire from both sides. I would suggest that Jean Monnet, the father of the European Common Market, is a useful model for future leaders. When there were conflicting purposes Monnet saw the possibility of shared goals, and he knew how to move his contemporaries toward those shared goals.

PRESERVING TRUST

A great deal depends on the general level of trust in the organization or society. The infinitely varied and complex doings of the society—any society—would come to a halt if people did not trust other people most of the time—trust them to observe custom, follow the rules, and behave with some predictability. Countless circumstances operate to diminish that trust, but one may be sure that if the society is functioning at all, some degree of trust survives.

Leaders can do much to preserve the necessary level of trust. And the first requirement is that they have the capacity to inspire trust in themselves. In sixteenth-century Italy, where relations among the warring kingdoms were an unending alley fight, Machiavelli's chilling advice to his prince— "It is necessary . . . to be a feigner and a dissembler," or, as another translator renders the same passage, "You must be a great liar and hypocrite"—may have been warranted.[7] And, under conditions of iron rule, Hitler and Stalin were able to live by betrayals. But in our society, leaders must work to raise the level of trust.

EXPLAINING

Explaining sounds too pedestrian to be on a list of leadership tasks, but every leader recognizes it. People want to know what the problem is, why they are being asked to do certain things, why they face so many frustrations. Thurman Arnold said, "Unhappy is a people that has run out of words to describe what is happening to them."[8] Leaders find the words.

Leaders explain. They teach and they sell. Those words sound too mundane to describe the lofty task of leadership but if leaders aren't teaching and selling, they're not leading.

—Speech at the Leadership Center of St. Louis, St. Louis, Missouri, 1994

To be heard above the hubbub in the public forum today, explaining generally requires more than clarity and eloquence. It requires effective access to the media of communication or to those segments of the population that keep ideas in circulation—editors, writers, intellectuals, association leaders, advocacy groups, chief executive officers, and the like.

The task of explaining is so important that some who do it exceptionally well play a leadership role even though they are not leaders in the conventional sense. When the American colonies were struggling for independence, Thomas Paine was a memorable explainer. In the powerful environmentalist surge of the 1960s and '70s, no activist leader had as pervasive an influence on the movement as did Rachel Carson, whose book *Silent Spring* burst on the scene in 1963.[9] Betty Friedan's *Feminine Mystique* played a similar role for the women's movement.[10]

Leaders teach. Lincoln, in his second inaugural address, provided an extraordinary example of the leader as teacher. Teaching and leading are distinguishable occupations, but every great leader is clearly teaching—and every great teacher is leading.

SERVING AS A SYMBOL

Leaders are inevitably symbols. Workers singled out to be supervisors discover that they are set apart from their old comrades in subtle ways. They try to keep the old camaraderie but things have changed. They are now symbols of management. Sergeants symbolize the chain of command. Parish religious leaders symbolize their churches.

In a group threatened with internal strife, the leader may be a crucial symbol of unity. In a minority group's struggle to find its place, combative leaders—troublesome to others—may be to their own people the perfect symbol of their anger and their struggle.

The top leader of a community or nation symbolizes the group's collective identity and continuity. For this reason, the death of a president produces a special reaction of grief and loss. Americans who were beyond childhood when John F. Kennedy was assassinated remember, despite the passage of decades, precisely where they were and what they were doing when the news reached them.

Thomas Jefferson became such a powerful symbol of our democratic aspirations that for generations politicians fought over his memory. Those who favored Hamiltonian views sought bitterly and unsuccessfully to shatter the Jefferson image. As Merrill Peterson has cogently argued, the man himself lost reality and the symbol took over.[11]

Outside the political area, Albert Schweitzer, the gifted theologian and musician who in 1913 gave up a comfortable and respected life in his native Germany to spend the remainder of his years presiding over a medical mission in Equatorial Africa, stands as the pristine example of leader as symbol.

Some individuals newly risen to leadership have a hard time adjusting to the reality that they are symbols. I recall a visit with a young college president who had just come into the job fresh from a professorship, with no prior administrative experience. He confided that he was deeply irked by an incident the preceding day. In his first speech before faculty, students, trustees and alumni he had simply been himself—a man of independent mind full of lively personal opinions—and many of his listeners were nonplussed and irritated. They were not interested in a display of idiosyncratic views. They had expected him to speak as their new leader, their symbol of institutional continuity, their ceremonial collective voice. I told him gently that they had expected him to be their spokesman and symbol, and this simply angered him further. "I'll resign," he said, "if I can't be myself." Over time, he learned that leaders can rarely afford the luxury of speaking for themselves alone.

Most leaders become quite aware of the symbolic aspects of their roles and make effective use of them. One of the twentieth-century leaders who did so most skillfully was Gandhi.[12] In the issues he chose to do battle on, in the way he conducted his campaigns, in the jail terms and the fasting, in his manner of dress, he symbolized his people, their desperate need, and their struggle against oppression.

Needless to say leaders do not always function as benign symbols. In the Iran-Contra affair of 1986–87 it became apparent that men bound by their oath of office were lying to the public, lying to the Congress of the United States, and lying to one another. To some Americans they became symbols of all the falsehoods and betrayals committed by a distant and distrusted government.

REPRESENTING THE GROUP

In quieter times (we love to imagine that there were quieter times) leaders could perhaps concentrate on their own followers. Today, representing the group in its dealings with others is a substantial leadership task.

It is a truism that all of the human systems (organizations, groups, communities) that make up the society and the world are increasingly interdependent. Virtually all leaders at every level must carry on dealings with systems external to the one in which they themselves are involved—tasks of representing and negotiating, of defending institutional integrity, of public relations. As one moves higher in the ranks of leadership, such chores increase.

It goes without saying that people who have spent their careers the world of the specialist or within the boundaries of a narrow community (their firm, their profession) are often ill-equipped for such leadership tasks. The young potential leader must learn early to cross boundaries and to know many worlds. The attributes that enable leaders to teach and lead their own constituencies may be wholly ineffective in external dealings. Military leaders who are revered by their troops may be clumsy with civilians. The business leader who is effective within the business culture may be lost in dealing with politicians. A distinctive characteristic of the ablest leaders is that they do not shrink from external representation. They see the long-term needs and goals of their constituency in the broadest context and they act accordingly. The most capable mayors think not just of the city but of the metropolitan area and the region. Able business leaders are alert to the political climate and to world economic trends.

The most remarkable modern example of a leader carrying out the representative function is Charles DeGaulle. DeGaulle has his detractors, but none can fail to marvel at his performance in successfully representing the once and future France-as-a-great-power at a time when the nation itself was a defeated, demoralized, enemy-occupied land. By his own commanding presence, he kept France's place at the table through the dark days. Years later Jean Monnet wrote: "It took great strength of character for him, a traditional soldier, to cross the great dividing line of disobedience to orders from above. He was the only man of his rank with the courage to do so; and in the painful isolation felt by those Frenchmen who had decided to continue the Allied struggle, DeGaulle's rare example was a source of great moral strength."[13]

RENEWING

Leaders need not be renewers. They can lead people down old paths, using old slogans, toward old objectives. Sometimes that is appropriate. But the world changes with disconcerting swiftness. Too often the old paths are blocked and the old solutions no longer solve anything. DeGaulle, writing of France's appalling unpreparedness for World War II, said: "The Army became stuck in a set of ideas which had had their heyday before the end of the First World War. It was all the more inclined that way because its leaders were growing old at their posts, wedded to errors that had once constituted their glory."[14]

Leaders must foster the process of renewal.

———

So much for the tasks of leadership. The individual with a gift for building a leadership team may successfully delegate one or another of those tasks to other members of the team. One function that cannot be delegated is that of serving as symbol. That the leader is a symbol is a fact, not a matter of choice. The task is to take appropriate account of that reality and to use it well in the service of the group's goals.

Another function that cannot be delegated entirely is the envisioning of goals. Unless the leader has a sense of where the whole enterprise is going and must go, it is not possible to delegate (or carry out personally) the other functions. To have "a sense of where the whole enterprise is going and must go" is, I am inclined to say, the very core and essence of the best leadership.

In a discussion of the tasks of leadership, a colleague of mine said, "I do not see 'enabling' or 'empowering' on the list. Aren't those the central tasks of leadership?" For those unfamiliar with contemporary discussions of leadership, I should explain that reference to *enabling* or *empowering* has become the preferred method of condensing into a single word the widely held conviction that the purpose of leaders is not to dominate nor diminish followers but to strengthen and help them to develop.

It is natural to suppose that those with undiscovered or undeveloped gifts are mainly the unfortunate of the world. But the loss occurs on a large scale in corporations, in government agencies, in nonprofits. It is surprising how many of these organizations make little or no effort to develop their human resources.

The goal is to offer people challenges favorable to the flowering of whatever gifts they may have—at whatever stage of the life cycle. We can remove the obstacles, unearth the buried gifts and release the world-renewing energies.

There are great untapped reservoirs of human energy and capacity awaiting leaders who can tap them, and societies that deserve them.

—*National Renewal*, 1995, p. 18

But enabling and empowering are not separable tasks. They require a variety of actions on the parts of leaders. For example:

- Sharing information and making it possible for followers to obtain appropriate kinds of education
- Sharing power by devolving initiative and responsibility
- Building the confidence of followers so that they can achieve their own goals through their own efforts
- Removing barriers to the release of individual energy and talent
- Seeking, finding, and husbanding the various kinds of resources that followers need
- Resolving the conflicts that paralyze group action
- Providing organizational arrangements appropriate to group effort

Any attempt to describe a social process as complex as leadership inevitably makes it seem more orderly than it is. Leadership is not tidy. Decisions are made and then revised or reversed. Misunderstandings are frequent, inconsistency inevitable. Achieving a goal may simply make the next goal more urgent: inside every solution are the seeds of new problems. And as Donald Michael has pointed out, most of the time most things are out of hand.[15] No leader enjoys that reality, but every leader knows it.

It would be easy to imagine that the tasks described are items to be handled separately, like items on a shopping list, each from a separate store. But the effective leader is always doing several tasks simultaneously. The best antidote to the shopping list conception is to look at the setting in which all the tasks are mingled—the complex interplay between leaders and those led.

The Heart of Leadership

All managers have subordinates, but that does not make them leaders with followers. "Executives are given subordinates: they have to earn followers." The heart of leadership involves the leaders' relationship with their followers, or constituents. It is a two-way exchange. "Good constituents make good leaders."

The relationship between leaders and followers varies from one culture to another. The relationship also varies according to whether the organization or group is in a time of quiescence or crisis, in prosperity or recession, on a steep growth curve or stagnating.

One tends to think of leaders as belonging in one category and followers in quite a separate category. But most of our leaders are followers in other contexts, and followers often perform leaderlike acts. The factory manager may be a leader locally but a follower in relation to the parent corporation. The college professor may be a leader in academic circles yet a follower in community affairs.

THE ROLE OF FOLLOWERS

Leaders are almost never as much in charge as they are pictured to be, followers almost never as submissive as one might imagine. That influence and pressure flow both ways is not a recent discovery. The earliest sociologists who wrote on the subject made the point. Max Weber (1864–1920), in discussing charismatic leaders, asserted that such leaders generally appear in times of trouble and that their followers exhibit "a devotion born of distress."[1] In other words, the state of mind of followers is a powerful ingredient in explaining the emergence of the charismatic leader.

Weber's great contemporary, Georg Simmel (1858–1918), was even more explicit, suggesting that followers have about as much influence on their leaders as their leaders have on them.[2] Leaders cannot maintain authority, he wrote, unless followers are prepared to believe in that authority. *In a sense, leadership is conferred by followers.* To say that followers have substantial influence on leaders sounds like the view of someone steeped in the democratic tradition. But Weber and Simmel were writing in pre–World War I Germany; their views were hardly the product of a populist environment.

Even monarchs and dictators have discovered that it is costly to take measures that offend the deeply held beliefs of their subjects, and that it is substantially less costly to attain their ends in ways that do not offend. Corporate executives learn comparable lessons today. They learn to operate within the framework of the culture, which is to say within the limits people in the system can accept in terms of their norms, beliefs and expectations. Leaders can go against the grain of the culture, but not without cost.

Contemporary research confirms the two-way character of the relationship.[3] It is this reciprocal aspect that underlies one of the soundest of political maxims: *Good constituents tend to produce good leaders.*

There is a striking difference between the situation of political leaders and that of line executives in business or government. In the political process, constituents have a measure of choice—and leaders must compete for approval. In corporate and governmental bureaucracies employees are supposed to accept their superiors in the hierarchy as their leaders. But, of course, quite often they do not. The assumption by line executives that, given their rank and authority, they can lead without being leaders is one reason bureaucracies stagnate. *Executives are given subordinates; they have to earn followers.*

STRUCTURE AND CONTROL

Whatever one may say about the influence of constituents, leaders continue to have a crucial role in the interaction. How should they play that role? It is a question that explodes into a thousand questions. Given our cultural framework, what patterns of leader-constituent interaction are most effective in accomplishing the purposes of the group? Does the group function most effectively when leaders make the decisions without consultation and impose their wills, or when they invite varying degrees of participation in the decision? The tension between the two approaches is nicely illustrated in a story (probably apocryphal) told of Woodrow Wilson when he was president of Princeton University. "How can I democratize this university," he demanded, "if the faculty won't do what I ask?"

Every leader willing to take risks has moments when he isn't sure whether his people are following him or chasing him.

—Journals

Should there be a high degree of structure in the relationship—a sharp differentiation between the roles of leaders and followers, a clear hierarchy of authority with emphasis on detailed assignments and task specifications? Or should the relationship be more informal, less structured, with leaders making the goals clear and then letting constituents help determine the way of proceeding?

Should there be an atmosphere of discipline, constraints, controls—in Navy parlance, a *tight ship*—or should there be autonomy, individual responsibility and freedom for growth, with the leader in the role of nurturer, supporter, listener and helper?

Should the leader focus on the job to be done—be *task-oriented* as the researchers put it—or should the leader be concerned primarily with the people performing the task, with their needs, their morale, their growth?

More than four decades of objective research have not produced dramatically clear answers to these questions, but they have yielded improved understanding of a set of very complicated relationships. American industry was puzzled when it became acquainted with the relationship between leaders and followers in Japanese industry in the 1970s, when Japan was beginning to outperform us in several industrial sectors. There would have been a lot more puzzlement if two generations of researchers had not enabled us to think in complex and imaginative ways about the leader-follower interaction, and prepared us to understand the alternatives to rigidly structured old-style leadership.

One reason simple answers have not emerged from the research is that there are no simple answers, only complicated answers hedged by conditions and exceptions. Followers do like being treated with consideration, do like to have their say, do like a chance to exercise their own initiative—and participation does increase acceptance of decisions. But there are times when followers welcome rather than reject authority, want prompt and clear decisions from the leader, and want to close ranks around the leader. The ablest and most effective leaders do not hold to a single style; they may be highly supportive in personal relations when that is needed, yet capable of a quick, authoritative decision when the situation requires it.

Some work environments are so rigidly structured that they destroy workers' initiative; others are so unstructured that the job never gets done. In the latter situation the workers themselves crave a clearer definition of goals, more orderly scheduling, better coordination and more precise assignments. Disorder is likely to produce demands for a more explicit framework of authority.

Again we must remind ourselves that in all these matters cultural differences exist. Studies comparing Americans with various European and Asian nationalities have consistently shown a greater inclination of Americans to favor individualism, equality and participation and to exhibit discomfort with hierarchy and status differences.

Living, Leading, and the American Dream

TWO-WAY COMMUNICATION

One generalization that is supported both by research and experience is that effective two-way communication is essential to proper functioning of the leader-follower relationship. It is a point that corporations have emphasized increasingly in recent years. There must be not only easy communication from leaders to constituents but also ample return communication, including dissent. Leaders, to be effective, must pick up the signals coming to them from constituents. And the rule is: If the messages from below say you are doing a flawless job, send back for a more candid assessment.

The huge, complex organizations we have fashioned and the sophisticated control systems devised to manage that complexity reduce the amount of face-to-face communication between leaders and led. And we pay a heavy price for the reduction. In interactions involving motivation, trust and loyalty, a message on the computer terminal is not enough. Suggestion boxes are not enough. Employee polls are not enough. Nothing can substitute for a live leader (not necessarily the top leader) listening attentively and responding informally. There is more to face-to-face communication than the verbal component. The leader's style, timing and symbolic acts all carry messages—and demonstrate that messages are being received. Wise leaders are continuously finding ways to say to their constituents, "I hear you." I once headed an agency with more than a hundred thousand employees and later led an organization with three hundred thousand members. The effort to deal face-to-face with as many as possible was exhausting but paid large dividends.

One hypothesis familiar to all who study leadership is that the leader gains by maintaining psychological distance from constituents—limiting access and accentuating status differences. DeGaulle is often cited as a proponent of this hypothesis. No doubt there are circumstances in which it is valid, but the research evidence is unclear.

THE MULTILEVEL DIALOGUE

In the most memorable conversations, the rational, verbal, conscious elements of the exchange are supplemented by communication at another level—nonrational, nonverbal, and unconscious. Words and sentences, tone of voice, body language, facial expression, timing, unfinished sentences, silences—all contribute to a multilevel dialogue. And so it is in the continuing conversation between leaders and followers.

Any social group, if it is more than a crowd of unrelated strangers, has shared needs, beliefs, aspirations, values, hopes and fears. The group creates norms that tend to control the behavior of its members, and these norms constitute the social order. It is in this context that leaders arise; and it is this context that determines what kinds of leaders emerge and what is expected of them. A loyal constituency is won when people, consciously or unconsciously, judge the leader to be capable of solving their problems and meeting their needs, when the leader is seen as symbolizing their norms, and when their image of the leader (whether or not it corresponds to reality) is congruent with their inner environment of myth and legend.

Effective leaders deal not only with the explicit decisions of the day—to approve a budget, announce a policy, discipline a subordinate—but also with that partly conscious, partly buried world of needs and hopes, ideals and symbols. They serve as models; they symbolize the group's unity and identity; they retell the stories that carry shared meanings. Their exemplary impact is great. There are messages for followers in what leaders pay attention to, in how they deal with critical incidents, in the correspondence between their words and acts, in the ethical tone of their behavior.

Truly gifted leaders know not only what constituents need but also what they fear, what they long to be, what they like best about themselves. Woodrow Wilson said, "The ear of the leader must ring with the voices of the people."[4]

To analyze complex problems, leaders must have a capacity for rational problem solving, but they must also have a penetrating intuitive grasp of the needs and moods of followers. The ablest leaders understand, rationally and intuitively, the expectations of people with respect to their leadership. And they are adept at meeting those expectations not only with rational verbal pronouncements but also with symbolic acts, ritual observances, and the like.

Living, Leading, and the American Dream

Obviously, the two-way communication is enhanced when leaders and constituents share deep cultural ties. The principle was brought home to me vividly some years ago when I boarded a train from Boston to New York and found myself surrounded by a spirited throng of Notre Dame fans en route to the Notre Dame–Army football game. One after another convivial stranger ("Hi, I'm Pat O'Toole!") urged me to join them in a festive drink. Then a buzz of excitement ran through the car—"He's coming!" And Boston's mayor, James Curley, made his way through the crowd. Curley was for the Irish of his city a symbol of their political triumphs, their memories of struggle, and their traditions as a people. He neither resigned nor lost support when he spent six months of one mayoral term in jail for mail fraud. I had met the mayor on earlier occasions, but in that lively railroad car I had for the first time a moving glimpse of the cultural ties that bound him to his people and them to him.

That leaders and followers share a culture (that is, share norms and values) enhances communication between the two, but is not an unmixed blessing. When the system is in grave need of renewal, leaders who wear the same blinders as their followers may be of little help in renewing.

PERCEPTION AND REALITY

Leaders develop their styles as they interact with their constituencies. They move toward the style that seems most effective in dealing with the mixture of elements that make up their constituencies.

Conventional wisdom says that there is, on one hand, the public image of the leader as perceived by followers, and on the other hand, the reality of what the leader truly is. But many researchers agree that how the followers perceive the leader is also reality—and in matters of leadership a more important reality than what the leader is really like. To complicate matters further, it is apparent in the life histories of more than a few great leaders that the real person and the person perceived by followers gradually merged, so that the question "What was the real person like?" became increasingly irrelevant.

SHAPER AND SHAPED

The interaction outlined here, while quite familiar to those who study leadership, is at odds with many conventional notions. People who have not thought much about it are likely to believe that all influence originates with the leader, that the leader is the shaper, never the object of shaping by followers.

Having brought leaders down from that pedestal, one can all too readily fall into the opposite error of supposing that leaders are clay in the hands of followers. Not really. Leaders, because of their significant positions, because of their inevitable symbolic roles, because of their natural persuasive gifts, wield undeniable influence.

I have portrayed a relationship between leaders and constituents in which each is in some measure the shaper, and in some measure the shaped. Obviously the interaction does not always work in balance. Sometimes the leader rides roughshod over the expectations of the people. Sometimes leaders are trapped by their constituents. (Show me a legislator described as "the darling of the liberals" or "the darling of the conservatives," and I'll show you a legislator without options.)

Conflicting Demands

Many years ago Edmund Burke posed a memorable question: Should leaders in a representative form of government be no more than mirrors of their constituents' views, or should they arrive at their own best judgments, taking constituent opinion into account but not being bound by it? Burke himself was repelled by the first alternative because it left no room for the representative's own judgment and conscience. John Adams held a similar view. On one occasion when Adams was proposing unpopular legislation, he urged Congress not to be "palsied by the will of our constituents."

One is bound to admire the political figure who, when great principles are at stake, has the courage to defy his constituency. Sam Houston, hero of the Texas war of independence and one of the most colorful leaders this nation has ever produced, deliberately brought an end to his political career by opposing secession. In an unforgettable warning to his fellow Southerners, he said, "Let me tell you what is coming. You may after the sacrifice of countless millions of treasure and hundreds of thousands of precious lives, as a bare possibility, win Southern independence, if God be not against you. But I doubt it."[5]

Admirable, but aside from such fateful moments our system is based on the presumption that political figures are reasonably responsive to their constituents.

Pluralistic Pressures

For years even-handed political scientists pointed out that there is and must always be tension between the two positions described by Burke, and that living, breathing politicians would necessarily move back and forth between the two. But the conditions of contemporary life have made the question itself a bit antiquated. As pointed out earlier, the politician must ask not "What does my constituency want?" but "What do each of my many constituencies want?" The actions that endear the leader to one constituency may anger another. Thus do the forces of a pluralistic society encourage the leader to show different faces to different constituencies or one enigmatic face to all.

One familiar and cynical view of leadership is that leaders do not lead the parade, but find out where it is going and get out ahead of it. For most leaders today, however, the single parade moving on an identifiable path is an anachronism. There are groups of constituents scurrying in every direction.

Beyond that, elected representatives must cope with the participation in the political process today of innumerable highly organized interest groups, many of them capable of bringing great benefit or harm to legislators and therefore capable of exerting great pressure on them. So legislators must consider the needs of their multiple constituencies, the demands of powerful interest groups, and finally, one hopes, their own best judgment.

One would like to think that somehow the resulting equation could be worked out in a manner compatible with integrity and sound public policy. But all too many public figures, their judgment befuddled by conflicting pressures or their character eroded by sell-outs, fail the test.

It is foolish to put all the blame on politicians. Each special interest represents a segment of the American people, sometimes a very narrow segment, sometimes very broad. So most of us are in one way or another involved in the multiple pressures that create for our politicians a life of impossible choices. We may properly demand rectitude and deplore lapses of integrity, but we must not pretend we are not implicated.

The moral dilemmas posed by multiple constituencies are not peculiar to politics. For the leader of a private welfare agency, for example, the major constituency is presumably the needy people served, but the rewards for the leader may come from pleasing some other constituency—perhaps the donors, perhaps the agency's governing board.

Trust

There is much to be gained for any leader in winning the trust of constituents. A leader capable of inspiring trust is especially valuable in bringing about collaboration among mutually suspicious elements in the constituency. The trust the contending groups have for such a leader can hold them together until they begin to trust one another.

It is not easy to sort out the ingredients of trust in leadership. I recall the senior partner of a law firm stressing to younger men and women in his firm the importance of client trust. One ambitious young lawyer asked how one went about winning trust, and the senior partner said dryly, "Try being trustworthy."

One of the most important prerequisites for trust in a leader is steadiness. Reliability is not only ethically desirable, it is generally a practical necessity. A leader who is unpredictable poses a nerve-racking problem for followers. They cannot rally around a leader if they do not know where he or she stands. A businessman friend of mine, commenting on his congressman, said, "It isn't that he's crooked, it's just that I can't keep track of him. He's too swift for me—I wish he'd stay in one place."

For leaders seeking to win trust, another requirement is fairness—fairness when the issues are being openly adjudicated, and, equally important, fairness in the back room. Contending elements seek private access to the leader, and if it is widely believed that such offstage maneuvering works, the system is in a constant turmoil of suspicion. Nothing is more surely stabilizing than confidence that the leader is unshakably fair in private as well as in public.

In public leadership another element in trust is reflected in the question, "Is this person one of us—our ethnic group, our social class, our economic level, our religion?" It is not a criterion that philosophers of democracy like to think about, but every observer of politics recognizes it.

A factor that undermines the trust of constituents in their leaders today is the set of practices that someone has described as the engineering of consent. Political managers, through skilled use of the media, convey as reality whatever illusion suits their purposes.

Before condemning the practice, as I intend to do, let us acknowledge that the media illusionists are not introducing an unknown ingredient into the political mix. It is not new for leaders to polish up their image, nor is it new that what followers perceive to be real diverges from reality. Hobbes said that the reputation of power is power. Leaders understand. If Merlin of King Arthur's court were to reappear and say to all leaders, "Your followers have many misconceptions about you and I can eliminate all such misconceptions with a wave of my wand," most leaders would consider it a dreadfully risky proposition. They know that many of the misconceptions are to their advantage—perhaps fostered by them. Nor are followers sternly in love with truth. A great many prefer an illusion that comforts them to a reality that breeds anxiety.

What contemporary political media consultants have introduced is not a new art but an old art so highly developed that it changes the very nature of the political process. It works, but like all high-powered advertising that falsifies, it engenders a mixture of short-term acceptance and long-term cynicism. Successful seduction is one thing. Winning trust for a system that repeats endlessly the cycle of seduction and exploitation is something else.

STRENGTHENING FOLLOWERS

If both leaders and constituents are significant actors in the relationship, we must talk not only about failures of leadership but also about failures of followership. There is a vast literature on the failures of leadership—on the abuse of power, injustice, indecisiveness and shortsightedness. Who will write the essay on individual and collective failures among followers? When it is written the essay will have to cover two matters at some length.

The most gifted leaders understand that the needs of people cannot be fully plumbed by asking them what they want or why they want it. One of the deepest truths about the cry of the human heart is that it is so often a cry that is never uttered. There are needs and feelings we express quite openly; lying deeper are emotions we share only with loved ones, and deeper still the things we tell no one. We die with much unsaid. It is strange that members of a species renowned for communicative gifts should leave unexpressed some of their deepest yearnings, their smoldering resentments, their worries and secret hopes, their longing to serve a higher purpose.

As a consequence, beneath the surface of most constituencies are dormant volcanoes of emotion and motivation.

The greatest poets, novelists and playwrights have always tapped those underground sources. They have always given expression to the unexpressed, have always had transactions with the hidden element in the souls of their audiences. The ablest leaders share that gift of understanding and carry on similar transactions. So do the most inspired religious teachers.

Some of the dormant emotions can be extremely destructive. But leaders should know what is there.

—*On Leadership,* 1990, p. 186

First, there are qualities such as apathy, passivity, cynicism, and habits of spectator-like noninvolvement that invite the abuse of power by leaders. Bertrand de Jouvenel said, "A society of sheep must in time beget a government of wolves."

Second, there is the inclination of followers in some circumstances to collaborate in their own deception. Given the familiar fact that what people want and need often determines what they see and hear, the collaboration comes easily. But a citizenry that wants to be lied to will have liars as leaders. Have we not tested that generalization at every level of government?

Rather than dwell on the failings, we would do well to focus on how to ensure better performance. Perhaps the most promising trend in our thinking about leadership is the growing conviction that the purposes of the group are best served when the leader helps followers to develop their own initiative, strengthens them in the use of their own judgment, enables them to grow and to become better contributors. Industrial concerns are experimenting with such an approach because of their hard-won awareness that some matters (for example, quality control, productivity, morale) simply cannot be dealt with unless lower levels of leadership are actively involved. To the extent that leaders enable followers to develop their own initiative, they are creating something that can survive their own departure. Some individuals who have dazzling powers of personal leadership create dependency in those below them and leave behind a weakened organization staffed by weakened people. Leaders who strengthen their people may create a legacy that will last for a very long time.

I have already pointed out that the interaction between leaders and constituents or followers does not take place in a vacuum. It is embedded in a historical or cultural context. It has an institutional setting. And these surrounding circumstances substantially affect not only the nature of the interaction but also the leadership attributes that are effective.

PART FIVE

Renewing
Our Society

The American Experiment

At the time of his death in 2002, John W. Gardner was immersed in an exploration of the attitudes, beliefs, and practices that can restore social wholeness while incorporating diversity. *The American Experiment* began as an essay. Edited down, it became a speech in 1998. In true Gardner fashion, it did not stop there. As the exploration continued, the piece changed subtly. What is here presented is the last version, edited in 2001. Reminding us that both Jefferson and Madison described our new nation as an "experiment," Gardner says, "The experiment is still in progress." Americans in all their diversity "are all working on the same quilt."

Think of humankind's search for social forms that honor liberty, justice and the worth and dignity of every person as a long, long story. It must have begun in fumbling, inarticulate ways tens of thousands of years ago. As Americans we have particular interest in the part of the story that began some two and a half centuries ago in the British colonies on the eastern coast of North America.

In the phrase "We, the people . . ." our Constitution expressed the revolutionary idea that "the people" could set up "governments of their own, under their own authority." It doesn't sound revolutionary today, but it astonished eighteenth-century Europeans. In the years from 1776 through 1791 most of the fundamental principles of our society were expressed. The great phrases echo in our minds—the consent of the governed . . . equality . . . the blessings of liberty . . . the establishment of justice. . . .

Those are only some of the extraordinary objectives laid out in the morning of the Republic. Those who fashioned the phrases were fully conscious that their efforts were the latest chapter in a story that reached back to the world of antiquity; and most of them were well aware of the writings of such later thinkers as Locke and Montesquieu.

DIFFICULTIES AHEAD

They knew they were setting high goals. In the *Federalist Papers,* James Madison candidly admitted that it was "a political experiment," that it depended "on the capacity of mankind for self-government." Thomas Jefferson also referred to it as "an experiment." And Alexander Hamilton said, "It seems to have been reserved to the people of this country by their conduct and example to decide . . . whether societies of men are really capable or not of establishing good government from reflection and choice, or whether they are forever destined to depend, for their political constitutions, on accident and force."

But one doubts that even the most farsighted spokesmen for the American Experiment could have envisioned the difficulties that lay ahead. After Jefferson's brave declaration that "all men are created equal" it took eighty-seven years and a bloody civil war to free the slaves, and another fifty-seven years before "We, the People," gave women the vote.

We need not list all the hard-won victories. Lincoln contributed unforgettably. Susan B. Anthony and Elizabeth Cady Stanton sparked the nineteenth-century battle for women's rights. Samuel Gompers, an immigrant, stabilized the labor movement. Andrew Carnegie, born in Scotland the son of a poor Scots weaver, became one of America's industrial pioneers and wrote an important chapter in America's philanthropic tradition. In the 1930s and 1940s Thurgood Marshall and his colleagues crafted the legal victories that laid the ground for the 1954 Supreme Court decision on school desegregation, and then Martin Luther King Jr. transformed the race issue from a legal battle to a popular movement. Betty Friedan touched off the mid-twentieth-century struggle for women's rights. La Donna Harris, Ada Deer, John Echohawk and others put the rights of Native Americans on the agenda. Cesar Chavez gave voice and power to the Hispanic farm workers of California.

There were (and are) many others, but those make the case. Men and women of many races and cultural origins have laid shaping hands on the American Experiment—and are still doing so. Many of those who have worked on the Experiment in the past half-century think of themselves as dissidents or critics. It doesn't occur to them that they are working on the same quilt, that they have joined the large and diverse group that is still writing the long story.

THE DISCONNECTION

Surveying the national scene today, one sees much that should put the American people in a good mood: the economy is healthy, unemployment is low and the cold war has ended. But they are not in a good mood. One remembers the cartoon of the worried-looking little girl tagging after her parents at Disneyland and asking: "Are we having fun yet?" For Americans generally the answer is "Not really." They are worried about the schools, about violent crime, about political corruption, about the growing gap between rich and poor, and most of all about the unraveling of the social fabric. There is a disconnection between the people and their leaders. Citizens do not trust their government. And a variety of polls indicate that the distrust extends to corporations and the media. People do not feel that they have much control over their lives, and the sense of impotence grows like a great life-endangering tumor.

We are treading the edge of a precipice here. Civilizations die of disenchantment. If enough people doubt their society, the whole venture falls apart. We must never let anger, fashionable cynicism or political partisanship blur our vision on that point. We must not despair of the Republic.

DISINTEGRATION OF COMMUNITY

The unraveling of the social fabric that we see today is legitimate cause for worry. A society, with its thriving institutions and great ventures, its power structure, its enormous capacity to reward and punish, may seem like a huge, unshakable edifice. But it is built on intangibles—a web of mutual obligations; shared beliefs, religious and secular; laws and customs; agreed-upon processes of governing; caring, trust and responsibility. Weaken those beyond a certain point and the great edifice—to quote Prospero in *The Tempest*— "melts into air, into thin air."

The intangible bonds of society hold within bounds the savagery of which humans are capable, ensure order, and make possible the accomplishment of shared purpose. When the web of community unravels, fearful things happen. Children gunning down children in the schoolyard. The daily news offers countless grim examples.

Some observers, perceiving the element of moral disintegration in the unraveling, leap to the conclusion that the teaching of moral values is the only necessary ingredient for recovery. But moral values are not created by people who give lectures on moral values. Moral values are inseparable from family and community, and the necessary ingredient for recovery is the rebuilding of community. Values are the fruit of the tree. If the apple trees are gone, don't expect apples. That is the prime reason for rebuilding community—not to re-create a cozy and nostalgic neighborliness but to provide the mutual obligations, social controls, trust and responsibility that are generated in family and community.

We are beginning to see that in our glorification of the unrestrained self, we forgot that the achievement of our shared goals (establish justice, promote the general welfare, secure the blessings of liberty, and the rest) depends on some measure of social cohesion. What we need is a reasonable balance between the claims of individuality and the claims of community.

REBUILDING COMMUNITY

The time-honored reaction to social disintegration is handwringing and despair. But the more one reads of history and anthropology the more one stands in awe of the human gift for generating and regenerating value systems, moral orders, institutions and societies. We have an uncelebrated capacity to counter disintegration with new integrations.

We must strive to preserve the family. The most common roots of a sense of community are in family life, when parents instill in children a sense of responsibility—for other individuals and for the group. The future vitality of one's community depends on the sense of responsibility of its citizens. If they don't care, all the experts in the world and all the money in the world won't help. Experts and money may patch up this or that specific problem. But they will be building on sand.

We must continue the work of community building in school, congregation, neighborhood, workplace. It's not just that we shall be building communities. We shall be developing citizens who know out of their own intimate experience the disciplines and satisfactions of community. They will understand teamwork, the observance of shared values, collaborative problem solving and the building of trust. In currently fashionable terms, we shall be building social capital.

This is not the place to explore in depth the ingredients of community. But one aspect is crucial: the requirement that we bring into being a wholeness that incorporates diversity. In a practical setting, this requires measures that enable diverse groups to know one another. It requires techniques of conflict resolution, coalition building and collaborative problem solving. It requires institutions that transcend group differences. The achievement of wholeness that incorporates diversity is the transcendent task for our generation, at home and worldwide. In this as in so many other things, our perspective must be global. But we cannot play a responsible role in the world if our homeland is riven in mind and spirit.

This is not an exercise in nostalgia. We can't look back to the old comfortable communities. We must—with respect for our tradition and a keen sense of present realities—build new communities for the tumultuous world ahead. But no matter what technology brings, we shall find ourselves returning to family, school, church, workplace and neighborhood—not because they are familiar and traditional but because they are the natural face-to-face settings where people can learn the lessons of responsibility, trust, caring and mutual obligation.

CITIZEN INVOLVEMENT

Americans have reason for negative attitudes today. But the sad, hard truth is that at this juncture the American people themselves are part of the problem.

Cynicism, alienation and disaffection will not move us forward. We have major tasks ahead. Our rate of violent crime is *several times* greater than that of other advanced industrial societies, and we fall behind most of them in providing for child care, parental leave, child immunization and access to medical care. A powerful thrust of energy will be needed to deal with these and other domestic problems, to say nothing of menacing international problems. Citizens—"We, the people"—will have to have the confidence and commitment to provide that energy.

The loss of civic faith is an obstacle. One might imagine that the solution would be for government to make itself worthy of our faith. But the plain truth is that the government (and other powerful institutions) will not become worthy of trust until citizens take positive action to hold it to account. Citizen involvement comes first.

It is not a liberal or conservative issue. It is not Democrats versus Republicans. It is a question of whether we are going to settle into a permanent state of alienated self-absorption or show the vigor and purpose that becomes us. We do not want it said that after a couple of great centuries we let the American Experiment disintegrate.

A fortunate by-product of citizen involvement is that when citizens become involved their morale improves. One cannot emphasize too strongly that a prime ingredient in the citizen's negative mood is the sense of disconnection. Anything that repairs the connection will help alter the mood. I recently encountered a friend of mine, a corporate CEO, wearing a hard hat and working with a neighborhood group on a Habitat for Humanity project. He said to me, "I can't solve the world's problems, but I can help build these houses. It's a great satisfaction."

THE GOOD NEWS

The good news is that there are grounds for hope, despite the negative mood reflected in the polls. Extraordinary things are happening at the grass roots in city after city across the nation—so extraordinary that I believe we are about to write a whole new chapter in the tumultuous American story. In fact the chapter is already being written.

In virtually every field of domestic problem solving—job training, family preservation, community-oriented policing, affordable housing, urban design, education, transportation, environment, economic development—there is a wave of innovation such as we have not seen for decades. New solutions to old problems, new ways of thinking about our urban dilemmas—they are all out there.

The cities and their metropolitan areas have a long way to go. But the heartening aspect is the sheer spirit and determination of the problem solvers who are driving the wave of innovation. Just that they exist is a beacon of hope for the rest of the nation. Don't pray for a burst of renewal. It is out there. We may not see it because the media do not always do justice to constructive grassroots problem solvers. One of our many chores is to remedy that. It's essential that we spotlight them, talk about their victories and disseminate the lessons they have learned.

DISPERSING INITIATIVES AND RESPONSIBILITY

The likelihood of citizen involvement will be considerably enhanced by the recent movement toward local initiative. Thirty years ago in a speech in Grand Rapids, I emphasized the importance of the local level: "We must provide increased opportunities for people to participate . . . we must restore a sense of community; and we must foster a sense of responsibility . . . all three aims depend on governmental arrangements that disperse power and initiative."

Today that is a very fashionable sentiment under the label of *devolution.* In the early 1970s, when we found that we were meeting formidable economic competition from Japan and West Germany little more than twenty-five years after those nations had suffered total military defeat, U.S. corporations undertook a reexamination of their own structure and practices. One of the principles that emerged was the necessity, in large-scale systems, of dispersing initiative and responsibility downward and outward. Too many centrally generated solutions—one-size-fits-all—rigidify the system and result in a loss of motivation and creativity at the periphery.

As applied to government, the concept of devolution does not mean the dismantling of Washington, as some extreme conservatives imply.

The federal government must continue to play an important funding role and federal agencies must foster the decision-making capacities and creativity of lower governmental levels. The American governmental system won't function at its best unless all levels—federal, state and local—are strong and vital, each performing functions appropriate to its level.

We must end the indiscriminate trashing of government. Carefully targeted criticism is immensely important, but mindless trashing has made able civil servants—who constitute the majority—feel like members of a battered profession. If we want to make government better, that is not the way to do it. Rather we must target our efforts. We must insist, for example, that government make itself worthy of respect by eliminating the many ways in which moneyed interests coerce legislators. In a land where the Founders committed themselves to the consent of the governed, the fact that money can buy political outcomes is an obscenity. The simple rule is, *"Hold power accountable."* We can no longer tolerate any government— federal, state or local—that has created such an impenetrable web of power, money and special interest that it is no longer controllable by the electorate.

KNITTING TOGETHER

In most cities, there is a striving toward new patterns of collaboration— new partnerships—among government agencies (at all levels) and the private sector, profit and nonprofit. Everyone recognizes that municipal government working alone cannot save the city. The most deteriorated parts of the city cannot save themselves. Collaboration is crucial.

But it is made more difficult by the existence of diverse segments of the population who don't know one another (and often don't want to). Race creates such divisions. The growing gap between rich and poor poses grave difficulties. We have noted the rift between affluent suburbs and deteriorating central cities. And there is resentment by many Americans of what they consider to be an emerging professional-executive-academic elite that always appears to be close to the levers of power.

In the face of such fragmentation, community building begins with open communication across boundaries. There must be candid and con-

Living, Leading, and the American Dream

tinued discussion in which resentments are pulled to the surface and each group comes to understand the assumptions and concerns of others.

One thing the cities are learning is that revitalizing a city requires leaders who can work cooperatively across boundaries; leaders who can work in *networks of responsibility* with all who share common goals; leaders who know how to listen to the voices of participants.

One of the most dependable ways to build community is to engage people in a common task. When individuals invest time and effort in the community it strengthens their ties to it. That is one of the many justifications for an ethic of voluntary community service.

A shared task that a number of American communities have already tested is one in which all segments of the populace come together to decide what they want the future of their community to be, and what are the priority tasks in getting there. Surprisingly, despite their internal diversity, most communities that have undertaken the exercise finally agree on a few important goals and priorities. They do not agree on everything, but they are not supposed to.

CONFLICT RESOLUTION

Very closely linked to collaboration is conflict resolution. The resolving of conflict has been a concern of diplomats and lawyers for centuries, but has taken new forms that have spread with astonishing rapidity in the last several decades. The purpose is not to abolish conflict, which is a normal part of human interaction, but to ensure a healthy outcome.

This is profoundly serious business. We must confront the awesome capacity of humans to be at one another's throats. We must tackle hatred and fanaticism in all their guises—racism, religious bigotry, political paranoia, and all other variations of divisive behavior. Not an easy task, looking at the performance of the species worldwide, looking at Bosnia, Rwanda and Oklahoma City, looking at the bloody scroll of history.

The techniques of conflict resolution and collaborative problem solving should be taught in every institution and every community. And there is much that can be done outside of formal conflict resolution processes to diminish the likelihood of conflict. A community that has created a network of healthy relationships that cut across ethnic lines, economic levels and religious differences has gone a long way toward making collaboration and conflict resolution possible. People from different ethnic, economic, and social groups tend to see each other in categories in stereotyped terms. With intelligently planned and continued interaction, categories and stereotypes fade and they begin to see one another as human beings. Each begins to understand that the others have different priorities, different notions of how the world works. Having achieved that, they can begin to talk seriously.

SHARED VALUES

The long-term task is to move toward some modest base of shared values. We do not want unanimity and our degree of agreement may be limited, but we must make the effort. Civilization is a drama lived in the minds of a people. It is a shared vision, shared norms, expectations and values. In today's climate, many Americans are so put off by the zealots in our national conversation that they are reluctant even to talk about values. But every successful society we know anything about has created a framework of law, custom and beliefs to channel behavior toward purposes deemed to be acceptable. The media have an understandable impulse to focus on our disagreements. But if we care about the American Experiment we had better search out and celebrate the values we share.

In seeking answers, we cannot draw uncritically from the past, nor can we reject the past. We must reject what was unworthy, build on the truths that are still vital in our tradition, face present challenges, however uncomfortable, and honor our profound obligation to the future.

COMMITMENTS BEYOND THE SELF

To make further progress toward those goals will require a commitment to the common good that has not been fashionable lately. Over the course of the twentieth century, perfect freedom for the individual became for many the ideal toward which to strive—the totally "liberated" self, not caught in a web of old-fashioned commitments, free to soar. Commitments beyond the self may involve hardship and self-sacrifice, but those who accept such commitments are spared the contemporary fate of rootlessness, hollowness and faithlessness. And they escape the ailment of the age: the tyranny of the imperious, imprisoning self. When we find meaning in the struggle, we are capable of heroic effort and endurance. Commitments not only discipline, they energize.

One can precipitate a lively debate by specifying the values toward which Americans aspire. Short of attempting a definitive list, it is possible to suggest the *kind* of items that might be included. *Justice, freedom* and *equality* would of course be on everyone's list. Equally certain to be endorsed by most Americans would be *personal integrity, the release of human possibilities, security of person, a sustainable environment* and *the values of community* (mutual support, caring, responsibility and citizenship).

Religious communities can and must contribute importantly to a more vibrant, unified and creative society. They can draw motivation from deep and ancient wells of belief. But those of us who care about the role of religion in our personal lives and in our national life must face a hard reality. Throughout the history of various religions there have occurred episodes of fanaticism, hatred, zealotry and violence. To give the help they can give in healing our society, religions must exorcise their own demons. Each religious person must exorcise the demons within. If we can heal ourselves, we can take on the great task of helping to heal the society.

VALUES IN ACTION

There is no possibility that moral, ethical or spiritual values can be preserved from one generation to the next if the only preservatives are words, monuments, rituals and sacred texts. The pastors of an earlier day sometimes complained that people sowed wild oats all week and then came to church on Sunday and prayed for a crop failure. Values live or die in the marketplace, the law offices, the family living quarters. The moral framework survives only when living men and women re-create the values for their own time—by living the faith, by caring, by doing. It is the universal ministry. It is true of religion; it is true of democracy; it is true of personal ethical codes. When ideals are torn loose from the earnest effort to approximate them, the words swirl endlessly and no one is enriched, no one bettered, no one saved.

It isn't enough to talk about respect for human dignity. What does it imply for employment and housing policy? It isn't enough to talk about the release of human possibilities. What does it imply for action in education and health? If these values are paramount, how should we comport ourselves? How should our institutions be designed? How should our government behave? What changes are called for in the real world? What can we do to help bring those changes about?

What must be done to make the key values an animating reality in our society today? We come back to the centrality of citizen involvement. Despite the promising wave of citizen activity mentioned earlier there is still—among all too many Americans—a fatal reluctance to lend themselves to any worthy common purpose. Appallingly low voter turnout is only one of the symptoms.

In World War I, I watched my grandmother knitting socks for soldiers, while my mother served as a volunteer nurse at the County Hospital. Neither of them saw themselves as exceptionally patriotic. Just about everyone was helping "the war effort." The same spirit was evident in World War II. A remarkably high percentage of the populace was contributing in some way—and enjoying it.

The Great Depression was a different sort of emergency, but again, there was an undeniable spirit in the populace. There was much hardship, and widespread misery but, somehow, beneath it all there was a hardy conviction that "We're going to see this thing through!"

Every local disaster—flood, hurricane, earthquake—evokes some of the same spirit. People want to help. They feel closer to one another. Sometimes one sees it in organizations, as in the Peace Corps in its early days.

What one sees in all these instances is a heightened commitment to shared purposes. No one imagines that we could achieve in peacetime the morale and motivation produced by enemy attack. But must we reconcile ourselves to the depths of demoralization one observes today? In a healthy free society most people must be involved *in some way.*

WHAT MUST WE DO?

First, citizens must inform themselves and engage in *deliberation* on the issues. Through public discussion, individuals from all segments of the community come to learn not only the substance of the issues but one another's beliefs, assumptions and preconceptions. All segments of the community must believe that their voice will be heard and listened to with respect. Citizens at every level must freely contribute.

In the past several years the most publicized form of citizen involvement has been *community volunteering*—citizens at work in one or another area of social service.

Advocacy is equally important. Voting is the most basic form, and low voter turnout is distressing. But advocacy extends far beyond the voting booth. Our national parks, the pure food and drug laws and the vote for women are testimony that successful citizen advocacy is well-rooted in our history. Government needs the goading and support that citizens can supply. Tough-minded politicians know that citizens can make a difference. More and more citizen groups such as Common Cause have learned to organize for advocacy.

Before we leave the subject of citizen engagement, we must remind ourselves that citizens also contribute in many ways that do not involve "civic affairs." All those who set standards for themselves, contribute to the well-being of their family, rear their children responsibly and accept individual responsibility are building the common future.

A great many of our cities have enough potential leadership talent to run a small nation, but the modern compulsion to specialize keeps most potential leaders in their well-upholstered niches in the professions, the corporate executive ranks and the universities. Who gave them permission to stand apart? Race and class distinctions keep other potential leaders segregated in their minority and working class neighborhoods. We must help potential leaders at all social levels to know and understand one another, and must persuade many to play roles of public leadership.

We owe a great deal to those of our forebears who climbed out of the trenches of specialization to public leadership. We forget that we were founded by a printer named Franklin, a plantation owner named Washington, a lawyer named Jefferson, a banker named Morris—to mention only a few. None of them had advanced degrees in statecraft. They trained themselves in order to create a new nation.

WHEN THE SPIRIT AWAKENS

Citizen engagement will not solve everything, but it is immensely important. Most of us are not Utopian. We do not dream of a perfect world. But we cannot abandon our efforts to make it less imperfect.

It is the fate of humans to face risks they cannot fully understand, much less control, to live in a world of complexities that frustrate purpose and tragedies that undermine morale. If there is any grandeur in the human struggle, it is in the capacity of considerable numbers of the species to fight on—buoyed by faith and hope—to surmount the setbacks, to envision gains beyond the losses and victories beyond the defeats, to pursue dreams in a world of bleak realities. That is not softheaded idealism. In the most hardheaded terms, that is the human task. In any generation, many have turned their backs on that task. Those who did not turn their backs went on to build civilizations. For them, neither optimism nor pessimism are appropriate words. They had courage; they had vitality; they had staying power.

So those who have not succumbed to the contemporary disaffection and alienation must speak the word of life to their fellow Americans. When the American spirit awakens it transforms worlds. But it does not awaken without a challenge. Citizens need to understand that this moment in history does in fact present a challenge that demands the best that is in them.

We can best gird ourselves for the path ahead by re-igniting some of the seminal, explosive ideas of the past: the ideas I've already listed and others—not least the old, great American idea of getting people off other people's backs—an idea we are still working on after all these years. The American Experiment is still in the laboratory. And there could be no nobler task for our generation than to move that great effort along.

Will Americans respond? I direct your attention to a trait shared by a great many citizens of this land. There is in them something waiting to be awakened, wanting to be awakened. Most Americans welcome the voice that lifts them out of themselves. They want to be better people. They want to help make this a better country.

When most of us were growing up the future beckoned. When my mother was a little girl living in a sod house on the plains of Nebraska, the future beckoned. When I was a boy in California during World War I, it beckoned. For Americans everywhere, the future was the repository of expectations and dreams—not just for ourselves but for humankind. Our minds were alive with possibility and hope. Let it happen again.

We are capable of so much that is not now asked of us. The courage and spirit are there, poorly hidden beneath self-interest and self-indulgence, left somnolent by the moral indifference of modern life, waiting to be called forth when the moment comes. Clearly, the moment has come.

Building Community

His studies on leadership led John W. Gardner to a study of community. He later commented: "Some of the problems of leadership today are problems of social cohesion. It's very hard for a leader to lead a non-community. A leader is constantly reaching down to those underlying values, that underlying stratum of shared values that he or she can work with to facilitate group purpose. And if the leader reaches down and there aren't any shared values, it's a real problem unless you've got machine guns. In a free society, you have to have those shared values. And that led me to community. I discovered that I had been dealing with aspects of it all along, clear back to *Excellence,* but I hadn't really asked myself what makes a community, what are the ingredients of community, why does it break down and what builds it up." The study led to *Building Community* (1993). What follows is a shortened version of that piece.

Families and communities are the ground-level generators and preservers of values and ethical systems. No society can remain vital or even survive without a reasonable base of shared values—and such values are not established by edict from lofty levels of the society. They are generated chiefly in the family, school, church, and other intimate settings in which people deal with one another face-to-face.

Where community exists it confers upon its members identity, a sense of belonging, a measure of security. Individuals acquire a sense of self partly from their continuous relationships to others and from the culture of their native place. But with today's mobility, and with family and community disintegration, many of those anchors for the sense of self no longer exist.

Without continuity of the shared values that community provides, freedom cannot survive. Freedom is not a natural condition. Habeas corpus, trial by jury, a free press and all the other practices that ensure our freedom are social constructions.

Strong and resilient communities can stand between the individual and any government that tries to impose dictatorial solutions from the right or left. Robert Nisbet[1]—and two decades later Berger and Neuhaus[2]—were quite right about the need for intermediary organizations and structures. Healthy communities constitute one kind of intermediary structure. Undifferentiated masses never have and never will preserve freedom against usurping power.

A community has the power to motivate its members to exceptional performance. It can set standards of expectation for the individual and provide the climate in which great things happen. It can pull extraordinary performances out of its members. The achievements of Greece in the fifth century B.C. were not the performances of isolated persons but of individuals acting in a golden moment of shared excellence.

Humans need communities—and a sense of community. A journalist resident in Los Angeles said of the youth gangs in that city: "Regrettably, they provide a sense of community that some of the kids can't find anywhere else." Part of an anti-gang strategy is to make sure the kids can find that sense of community somewhere else.

The historians, sociologists and anthropologists who did the first studies of peasant or tribal communities were immensely taken with the social cohesion, the wholeness, the solidarity of these human groupings, and for a long time they tended to idealize that image of community. Few communities in the United States today offer anything approaching that standard of cohesiveness. But many have within the memory of living persons supplied some of the same benefits—security, a sense of identity and belonging, a framework of shared assumptions and values, a network of caring individuals, the experience of being needed and more.

COMMUNITIES IN DANGER

Progressively the traditional community has been stripped of its autonomy and deprived of many of its functions. Today we see the weakening and collapse of communities of obligations and commitment, and of coherent belief systems. We see a loss of a sense of identity and belonging, of opportunities for allegiance, for being needed and responding to need—and a corresponding rise in feelings of alienation, impotence and anomie.

Families fall apart. People suffer isolation, alienation, estrangement. More and more lost and rootless people drift through life without a sense of belonging or allegiance to anything. Too many of them lack any supportive network. The rise of the so-called support group is no accident. Where can individuals turn to still their anxieties when there is no longer a web of reciprocal dependencies? The casualties stream through the juvenile courts and psychiatrists' offices and drug abuse clinics. And quite aside from individual breakdown, many of our contemporaries, freed by the disintegration of group norms, torn from their natural home in a context of shared obligations, have gotten drunk on self.

When a community disintegrates, the consequences for its members can be destructive. We have seen all the disorders of men and women torn loose from a context of community and shared values. Individuals often experience it as a loss of meaning, a sense of powerlessness. They lose the conviction that they can influence the events of their lives or the community (non-community) in which they live. And one striking consequence is a diminution of individual responsibility and commitment.

Those in the upper range of the economic and social scale are less conscious of the need for community. The consequences of community breakdown are far less vivid and violent in the areas where they live. They don't feel the same immediate threat to their lives and safety. Perhaps for those reasons, some social analysts think of community breakdown as chiefly a problem for the lower socioeconomic levels. But social disintegration is no less malignant when it occurs in an environment of physical comfort. Many of the gifted transgressors whose criminal activity has shattered public confidence in Wall Street and Washington have come from backgrounds characterized by affluent disintegration.

BEYOND THE TRADITIONAL COMMUNITY

Setting about the contemporary task of building community, one discovers at once that the old, beloved traditional model will not serve our present purposes. Nostalgia for "the good old days" will not help us through the turbulent times ahead.

The traditional community was homogeneous. Today most of us live with heterogeneity, and it will inevitably affect the design of our communities. Some of the homogeneity of traditional communities was based on exclusionary practices we cannot accept today.

The traditional community experienced relatively little change from one year to the next. The vital contemporary community will not only survive change but, when necessary, seek it.

The traditional community commonly demanded a high degree of conformity. Because of the nature of our world, the best of our contemporary communities today are pluralistic and adaptive, fostering individual freedom and responsibility within a framework of group obligation.

The traditional community was often unwelcoming to strangers, and all too ready to reduce its communication with the external world. Hard reality requires that present-day communities be in continuous and effective touch with the outside world, and our values require that they be inclusive.

The traditional community could boast generations of history and continuity. Only a few communities today can hope to enjoy any such heritage. The rest, if they are vital, continuously rebuild their shared culture and consciously foster the norms and values that will ensure their continued integrity.

In short, much as we may value the memory of the traditional community, we shall find ourselves building anew, seeking to reincarnate some of the cherished values in forms appropriate to contemporary social organization. The traditional community, whatever its shortcomings, did create, through the family, through the extended family and through all the interlocking networks of community life a structure of social interdependency in which individuals gave and received support—all giving, all receiving. With that no longer available, we must seek to reconstruct comparable structures of dependable interdependency wherever we can—in the workplace, the church, the school, and the youth-serving organizations.

FORMS OF COMMUNITY

Communities take many diverse forms today. Traditionally we have thought of a community as a geographically coherent and bounded place that was the scene of both work and home life. Such communities survive, but they aren't what they used to be. The small town of today is linked into economic networks that girdle the globe. The mobility and transience of its population makes cosmopolitanism inevitable. And every day, thanks to the media, the excitement and anxieties of a troubled world wash through it like a spring flood.

More common today is the pattern in which people form a geographically coherent residential community but have widely scattered places of work. This pattern, common among suburbs and bedroom communities, has been criticized by social commentators. Some flatly regard it as falling outside the definition of community; but it has to be counted as one of the forms that community is taking in the contemporary world. Some suburbs are communities in the best sense of the word.

There are some sites of common activity—work, worship, education—where people associate regularly but come from widely scattered residential sites. For a good many people these are the most authentic communities they know.

There are dispersed communities in which neither the residences nor the worksites of members are contiguous. The members might be scattered all over the nation (or the world) but are held together by occupational, religious or other bonds. Religious orders are perhaps the oldest example, professional societies the most common contemporary example. Perhaps dispersed groups can never achieve the full richness that we associate with the word *community*. Maybe they can survive as communities only if the members receive their initial indoctrination in face-to-face settings in which deeper bonding can occur—and if they periodically gather for "retreats" or reunions to reaffirm the bond.

Another model (of limited value) is the community of shared struggle. Bonding commonly occurs among individuals who are fighting a significant battle shoulder to shoulder—a strike, a protest, a natural disaster. Nations have been born in struggle, as have labor unions, political parties and veteran's organizations. But more commonly, the community born of struggle fades swiftly when the battle is over—unless those involved create the institutional arrangements and noncrisis bonding experiences that carry them through the year-in-year-out tests of community functioning.

Finally, a model that is decidedly useful but also decidedly limited is provided by small group bonding experiences. Ever since the National Training Laboratory began experimenting with small group behavior after World War II, it has been apparent that certain types of small group activity produce rather remarkable emotional bonding among the participants. It emerges from the shared confessions that occur in therapeutic or self-help groups. It occurs in the "ropes and rock climbing" exercises that are now a familiar part of many leadership training programs. It can produce a powerful effect. But it is a *bonding experience,* not a community.

The earliest communities studied—tribal and peasant communities—involved bonds of reciprocal dependency that were usually unchanging and unchangeable. The bonds were not a matter of choice. We have moved steadily toward choice. Present-day communities are characterized by ease of exit.

In the contemporary world, membership in one particular community does not preclude membership in other communities. Indeed, it is probably the norm that individuals have outside ties and interests, and many are full-fledged members of two or more communities (for example, one where they live, another where they work).

REGENERATION

Disintegration of human communities is as old as human history. Disease, natural disasters, conquest and absorption into emerging urban centers were the most common causes. But there were always processes of regeneration at work to counter disintegrative forces. As old social groupings broke down, new groupings tended to form. Humans are community-forming animals.

To cope with change, the process of value generation must go on continuously. The regenerative powers of human society have not weakened.

The capacity of humankind to create and re-create social coherence is always there—enduring and irrepressible.

But today communities are being continuously undermined and we cannot be optimistic about the outcome unless we take deliberate measures to abet the regenerative processes and slow the destructive processes. What is needed is active nurturing and rebuilding in a spirit that honors both continuity and renewal.

I think of community as a set of attributes that may appear in diverse settings—a school, a congregation, a town, a suburb, a workplace, a neighborhood. I'm going to list ten attributes of a community that would be viable in the contemporary world. There is no value neutrality in my description of the ingredients—but I believe the values explicit in these are widely shared. My interest is not in depicting Utopia. My interest is to get us away from vague generalizations and to identify some ingredients we can work on constructively.

Some methods buy community at too high a price, and I shall not advocate them. It is always possible, for example, to build community by creating (or exaggerating) an outside threat. Many cults force new members to divest themselves of old ties and to cast off old identities. Many totalitarian societies create community by cutting off other options for their members.

Wholeness Incorporating Diversity

In our system, "the common good" is first of all preservation of a system in which all kinds of people can—within the law—pursue their various visions of the common good *and* at the same time accomplish the kinds of mutual accommodation that make a social system livable and workable. The play of conflicting interests in a framework of shared purposes is the drama of a free society. It is a robust exercise and a noisy one, not for the fainthearted or the tidy-minded. Diversity is not simply "good" in that it implies breadth of tolerance and sympathy. A community of diverse elements has greater capacity to adapt and renew itself in a swiftly changing world.

But to speak of community implies *some* degree of wholeness. What we seek—at every level—is pluralism that achieves some kind of coherence, *wholeness incorporating diversity.* I do not think it is venturing beyond the truth to say that wholeness incorporating diversity is the transcendent goal of our time, the task for our generation—close to home and worldwide.

"Wholeness" does not characterize our cities today. They are seriously fragmented. They are torn by everything from momentary political battles to deep and complex ethnic rifts. Separate worlds live side by side but fail to communicate or understand one another. The list of substantive issues facing the city are not the city's main problem. Its main problem is that it can't pull itself together to act on *any* of the issues. It cannot think as a community or act as a community.

As we look at the world's grimmest trouble spots, wholeness incorporating diversity seems a hopeless quest. But there are a good many cities and even nations where markedly heterogeneous populations live and work together quite peaceably.

To prevent the wholeness from smothering diversity, there must be a philosophy of pluralism, an open climate for dissent, and an opportunity for subcommunities to retain their identity and share in the setting of larger group goals.

To prevent the diversity from destroying the wholeness, there must be institutional arrangements for diminishing polarization, for teaching diverse groups to know one another, for coalition-building, dispute resolution, negotiation and mediation. Of course the existence of a healthy community is in itself an instrument of conflict resolution.

A clear part of the problem—particularly in our cities—is the fragmentation of leadership. Most leaders are One Segment Leaders, fattening on the loyalty of their own segment and exhibiting little regard for the city as a whole. Indeed, sometimes they thrive on divisiveness. But in any city there are leaders capable of a broader perspective, capable of joining with leaders of other segments (in and out of government) to define and solve the larger problems of the community. Such networks of responsibility can serve as a kind of constituency for the whole.

A Reasonable Base of Shared Values

To require that a community agree on everything would be unrealistic and would violate our concern for diversity. But it has to agree on something. There has to be some core of shared values. Of all the ingredients of community this is possibly the most important. The values may be reflected in written laws and rules, in a shared framework of meaning, in unwritten customs, in a shared vision of what constitutes the common good and the future.

The community teaches. If it is healthy it will impart a coherent value system. If it is chaotic or degenerate, lessons will be taught anyway—but not lessons that heal and strengthen. We treasure images of value education in which an older mentor quietly instructs a child in the rules of behavior, but that is a small part of a larger and more turbulent scene. The child absorbs values, good and bad, on the playground, through the media, on the street—everywhere. It is the community and culture that hold the individual in a framework of values.

None of this should be taken to mean that healthy communities should suppress internal criticism or deny their flaws or agree on everything. Shared beliefs can become shared delusions. If the community is very lucky—and few will be in the years ahead—its shared values will be embedded in tradition and history and memory. But most future communities will have to build and continuously repair the framework of shared values. Their norms will have to be explicitly taught. Values that are never expressed are apt to be taken for granted and not adequately conveyed to young people and newcomers. Individuals have a role in the continuous rebuilding of the value framework, and the best thing that they can do is not to preach values but to exemplify them. Teach the truth by living it. All of us celebrate our values in our behavior. It is the universal ministry. The way we act and conduct our lives is saying something to others—perhaps something reprehensible, perhaps something encouraging.

Because we live with many faiths, we must foster a framework of shared secular values—liberty, justice, tolerance—while leaving people free to honor diverse deeper faiths that undergird those values.

Caring, Trust, and Teamwork

In some of the primitive tribes studied by anthropologists, the group was almost wholly self-sufficient. The community was responsible for all the functions essential to human life: the provision of food and shelter, the resolving of internal conflicts, common defense in a hostile environment (human and other), the passing on of survival skills as well as provision of a context of meaning, allegiance, identity and emotional fulfillment.

Today the community has been stripped of many of these functions by federal and state government, by distant suppliers and by media external to the community. All the more important then that we give attention to the functions that remain. Prominent among those remaining functions is providing the climate of caring, trust and teamwork that ensures the accomplishment of group purpose.

The members of a good community deal with one another humanely, respect individual differences and value the integrity of each person. A good community fosters an atmosphere of cooperation and connectedness. There is recognition and thanks for hard work, and an awareness by the members that they need one another. There is a sense of belonging and identity, a spirit of mutual responsibility. There is the altruism that is so consistently urged by major world religions.[3] There is trust and tolerance and loyalty. Everyone is included. There is room for mavericks, nonconformists and dissenters. There are no outcasts. Obviously, this describes an ideal community, perhaps beyond our reach. The best communities we know have a long way to go.

Research shows that much of the basis for positive and generous adult relationships traces back to a warm and nurturing environment in childhood. But there are measures that can be taken at the adult level.

In seeking the goal of caring, trust and teamwork, *the first necessary step is to give all subgroups and individuals reason to believe that they are fully accepted.* It is essential that ethnic minorities, women, newcomers, the disabled and other marginalized groups feel that they count. We know how to fight that battle and should not let up.

Another step—equally crucial—is to institutionalize arrangements for dispute resolution. Conflicting purposes and values are inevitable in our pluralistic society and part of the normal functioning of a healthy community. Some systems for resolving disputes have been institutionalized over centuries. Our courts, our representative political institutions and the economic marketplace resolve many conflicts. Some cities have community boards to deal with neighborhood disputes, commissions to work on racial harmony, or other instruments to diminish polarization.

Beyond that, the arts of reconciling conflicting purposes should be taught in every school and college in the world. The goal is not to abolish conflict, which is inevitable and even healthy, but to achieve constructive outcomes.

The third step is based on shared tasks. When individuals invest time and energy in their community, their bond with the community is strengthened. If they give something *to* (or give up something *for*) the community, they feel closer to it. Community problem-solving activities build community. A healthy community will provide ample opportunities for the individual to participate in community efforts.

Finally, a healthy community creates a considerable variety of bonding experiences. I have already mentioned some, such as the common task, but there are many others: shared social activities, ceremonies, celebrations, rituals, the honoring of exemplary figures or retelling the community story. Across the broad expanse of urban America today, the chief community bonding experiences are probably provided by religion and sports. Yes, sports.

Effective Internal Communication

Members of a well-functioning community communicate freely with one another. One of the advantages of the small group is that frequent face-to-face communication is possible. In large systems (cities and corporations, for example) conscious effort is needed to maintain a free flow of information among all elements of the system, and to combat the we-they barriers that impede the flow.

Groups that find themselves in disagreement should feel free to express their views. That is essential, but groups that fall into habits of fierce mutual accusation generally diminish communication—a condition that can be reversed by techniques of conflict resolution if both sides are willing to use them. A tradition of civility helps. A common language helps.

Formal provisions must be made for communication among subcommunities, but even better is a rich web of personal acquaintance cutting across the boundaries of subgroups.

In cities and towns, local government and the media have a positive responsibility for effective communication within the community, but they cannot be counted on as the only means. There should be active and continuous communication among a variety of organizations and agencies in and out of government. Nongovernmental organizations can develop effective information-sharing networks.

For the community as a whole, there should be occasions when members gather for public discussions. There must be organizations willing to provide meeting spaces or to serve as conveners for such community discussions.

Participation

A two-way flow of influence and communication is dictated by our value system. Our society requires a dispersed network of leaders spread through every segment of the organization and down through every level. And beyond this wide network of identified leaders, there will be, in a vital community, a large number of individuals voluntarily sharing those leadership tasks that lend themselves to sharing, for example, achieving a workable level of unity, motivating, explaining.

For a city perhaps the most important requirement for effective leadership is the continuous collaboration between city government and all the segments of private sector leadership, profit and nonprofit. Private sector groups are coming to recognize that such participation is a positive duty.

The citizen voting or speaking out in public meetings is participating, but so are the parents who rear their children with a sense of community responsibility, so is the teenager who volunteers to tutor disadvantaged children. The healthy community has many ways of saying to the individual, "You belong, you have a role to play, and the drama has meaning." It is this more than anything else that accounts for the sense of identity so characteristic of community members.

We need a sound educational system that includes preparation for effective leadership and participation. The overwhelming emphasis in contemporary education on individual performance *must* be supplemented with education in the accomplishment of group purpose. Some of the new cooperative education programs achieve that result. At some point in high school and college, one or another form of community service or political internship is helpful.

Many other institutions in the community can help with the task of civic education. Any citizen group, any advisory commission, every civic task force is a potential training ground for leaders and community builders. In addition, the community should have one or another form of "community leadership program" of the sort sponsored by The National Association for Community Leadership or the American Leadership Forum. All segments of community leadership must be represented in such groups.

Affirmation

A healthy community reaffirms itself continuously. It builds its own morale. It may face up to its flaws and tolerate criticism, but basically it has confidence in itself. No group, no matter how well established, can take such affirmation entirely for granted. There are always young people to instruct and newcomers to welcome. Even a group with no history or tradition to build on can reaffirm its identity, its purposes and its shared values. Individuals are generally members of more than one community and have competing demands upon them. The communities that survive the competition are likely to be those that press their claims.

In an earlier era communities celebrated their beginnings, their roots. But in few American communities today can a majority—or even a sizable fraction of members—claim any link with the community's history. The story of most communities today is acceptance of wave upon wave of newcomers who over generations found a way of living with the culture, influencing it as they accommodated to it. The drama and pride of our communities has been the coming together of many cultures—with consequent enrichment of all.

Normally, communities have ceremonies and celebrations to reaffirm the symbols of group identity, recognize and reward exemplary members, and provide bonding experiences. In addition, there should be more formal measures to further civic education, not just in the schools and colleges but in the churches, youth organizations and civic groups. It is everybody's business.

Links Beyond the Community

The sound community has seemingly contradictory responsibilities: it must defend itself from the forces in the outside environment that undermine its integrity, yet it must maintain open, constructive and extensive relations with the world beyond its boundaries. The public school, for example, must be in some respects a haven for its students, capable of shutting out some of the most destructive aspects of city life, but it can maintain itself as a strong institution only through extensive community relations and constructive dealings with the school district and state.

A vital community inevitably distinguishes itself from it surroundings to *some* degree. If there were no boundaries at all, community members would not know where they belonged. But every community must combat the self-absorption that increases its distance from others. Total self-absorption is not acceptable. Impermeable boundaries are not acceptable.

The community seeks to preserve its own integrity while reaching out to play an effective part in a larger whole. In the most desirable outcome, the community's leaders will establish collaborative ties with leaders of other subcommunities. The well-functioning city has ties with its metropolitan area and its region—and with state and federal governments. Not only city government but leaders in the business and nonprofit worlds should participate in establishing the broader links.

The same may be said of the community development groups, neighborhood organizations and grassroots communities now flourishing. They can and should define their own problems and exercise their own initiative

Living, Leading, and the American Dream

in working toward solutions. But, finally, they must have recourse to larger networks—and must play their role in strengthening the larger systems.

There is no way for them to survive without many kinds of linkage into larger frameworks. And even if they were to survive they would be incapable of registering their concerns and playing their role without such linkage.

Development of Young People

Those who will lead the community four decades hence are scampering off to school today. Any community that seeks to ensure its continued vitality will not only enable those young people to develop to the full, it will prepare them for their future roles, instilling shared values, fostering commitment to shared purposes, and teaching them to preserve and renew the common heritage.

Beginning in elementary and high school, girls and boys should learn to take some responsibility for the well-being of any group they are in—a seemingly small step but, as I pointed out earlier, the first step toward community participation and leadership development. Cooperative education methods can help. On the playing field and in group activities in and out of school, teamwork can be learned. Through volunteer and intern experiences they learn how the adult world works and have the experience of serving their society. Every organization serving the community should find ways of involving young people.

A Forward View

A healthy community should have a sense of where it should go and what it might become. In an earlier era, when many communities experienced little change over decades, the idea might have made little sense. The answer might have been, "We're not going anywhere. We're happy where we are."

In theory, a community doesn't absolutely have to have a goal or vision beyond survival, physical and spiritual. It doesn't have to be going anywhere. But in practice, if it drifts it may have changes forced upon it that it would not have chosen. Today change is a given—for good or ill. So the questions become, Where will the currents of change take our community if we fail to act? How can we intervene to ensure a better outcome for our children and our children's children? Answers to these questions can provide a vital goal and focus of motivation. Far from pursuing such a goal, many of our communities today are laying up trouble for their children—in debt and in deteriorated infrastructure, to name only two.

The conventional community approach to the future is to think in terms of a planning commission. Because over the years such commissions have tended to get bogged down in routine activities, the preference recently has been for *ad hoc* exercises such as LA 2000—short-term, intensive, wide-focus efforts to identify future problems and prepare for them.[4] But such exercises should be supplemented by many dispersed institutional efforts. Local academic institutions should be engaged in continuous research relevant to the future of the community and its region. Various segments of the community—business, agriculture, education—should be examining economic and demographic trends relevant to their future.

Institutional Arrangements for Community Maintenance

Every community has institutional arrangements for group maintenance. In a city the most conspicuous arrangements are those we call government. In a nonprofit organization it is the board of trustees, the director and staff, and perhaps some volunteer committees. The forms are infinitely varied. Unwritten codes of conduct play their role.

There are marked variations from one community to the next in the extent to which the institutional arrangements are characterized by structure and control. We can't accept the extremes. Excessive community control does not accord with our ideal of individual freedom and responsibility. At the other extreme is a degree of anarchy that does not permit (or invite) the emergence of shared values, that tolerates a degree of disorder wholly incompatible with a sense of community. Between the extremes we can tolerate considerable variation in the degree of structure and control.

In a democratic society, a high proportion of the population has some role in the maintenance system. In a town, for example, there are leaders in town government and in the private sector. There are lower-level leaders in every segment of the community. And there are a considerable number of individuals throughout the system who "share leadership tasks" on their own initiative, working to maintain group motivation, to heal rifts, to do volunteer work. And then there are the many members who participate by voting, by setting an example of appropriate individual behavior, by nurturing younger members.

Some of the writers who are most concerned to restore a sense of community today are not inclined to pay much attention to government, but its role is critically important. If it doesn't work, it must be made to work. We cannot take it for granted. It has to be made an instrument of community and of participation, worthy of respect and trust. Politicians are much maligned, but the best of them, skilled in mediating among disparate groups, can make a significant contribution to community.

There must be continuous collaboration between local government and the private sector. There must be an infrastructure of neighborhood associations, churches, citizen groups, youth-serving organizations, and professional groups. Today some of these groups are genuinely interested in the community as a community, but most are highly specialized, each existing in its own little niche, rarely if ever thinking about the fate of the community as a whole. They must learn where their civic duty lies. They are an important part of the fabric of the community.

CONCLUSION

Social theorists have pointed out that among the first acts of totalitarian dictators upon coming to power is to undermine the private associative links of the citizenry, so there is nothing left but the State and a mass of separate individuals, easily dominated. Such theorists argue (correctly) that the close-in loyalties—to family, school, church, lodge, union, neighborhood and community—are essential to the health of a free society. Not only do such loyalties make the rise of an absolutist state far more unlikely, they are teaching arenas for the arts of community that we need so desperately at national and world levels.

An understanding of the mutual dependence of individual and group has existed below the level of consciousness in all healthy communities from the beginning of time. But that understanding survives faintly if at all today. The contemporary self, insatiable in its quest for autonomy, all too often rejects custom and tradition and looks with contempt at the imperfect institutions of its own society. No society can survive such abandonment by its members. A sound society provides the individual with nurture in infancy, a secure environment in which to mature, a framework of meaning, a sense of identity and belonging—and sometimes much more. In healthy societies the individual gives something back—at the very least, allegiance and some measure of commitment to the society.

Liberty and duty, freedom and obligation. That's the deal. You are free within a framework of obligations—to your family, to loved ones, to community, nation, species; in Shaw's words, to "the posterity that has no vote and the tradition that never had any"; to your God; to your conception of an ethical order. The obligations you accept may be different from mine. But it is not in the grand design that we can have freedom without obligation. Not for long.

The mutual dependence between individual and group is ancient. But today the survival of our communities—and our survival as social beings—requires that we alter somewhat the nature of the relationship. Historically the society supplied most of the continuity and coherence through its long-established belief-systems and nurturing institutions. In return the individual gave allegiance but—except in time of war—it was truly a rather passive allegiance. One accepted one's culture as an infant accepts its cradle.

Passive allegiance isn't enough today. The forces of disintegration have gained steadily and will prevail unless individuals see themselves as having a positive duty to nurture and continuously reweave the social fabric.

The task is not one of uncritical reaffirmation; it is a task of renewal. And the process of renewal encompasses both continuity and change, reinterpreting tradition to meet new conditions, building a better future on an acknowledged heritage and the wisdom of experience. That calls for loving, nurturing critics.

Living, Leading, and the American Dream

We must seek to regenerate the sense of community from the ground up. Men and women who have come to understand, in their own intimate settings, the principles of "wholeness incorporating diversity," the arts of diminishing polarization, the meaning of teamwork and participation will be strong allies in the effort to build elements of community into the metropolis, the nation and the world.

It would be a grave mistake to imagine that—in a great burst of energy—we can rebuild our communities and then turn to other tasks. That assumes a degree of stability we once knew but may never see again in our lifetime. We can never stop rebuilding.

The communities we build today may eventually be eroded or torn apart by the crosscurrents of contemporary life. Then we rebuild. We can't know all the forms community will take, but we know the values and the kinds of supporting structures we want to preserve. We are a community-building species. We might become remarkably ingenious at creating new forms of community for a swiftly changing world.

18

Leading Community

As our communities become ever more diverse, leading them becomes both more difficult and more critical. To John W. Gardner the very diversity that makes leadership harder provides an opportunity to disperse leadership throughout the community. Leadership should be shared, and citizens should be able to participate in leadership. This selection is adapted from the twelfth leadership booklet Gardner wrote for INDEPENDENT SECTOR.

Leadership is dispersed throughout our society. Without thinking about it very analytically we have associated that fact with our notions of democracy and pluralism. But as our understanding of the principles of organization has developed, we have come to understand that there is really no alternative to such dispersal of leadership if large-scale systems are to retain their vitality.

The point is relevant not only for our society as a whole but for all the organized subsystems (corporations, unions, government agencies, and so on) that comprise it. Most leadership today is an attempt to accomplish purposes through (or in spite of) large, intricately organized systems.

There is no possibility that centralized authority can call all the shots in large and complex human systems, whether the system is a corporation or a nation. Individuals in all segments and at all levels must be prepared to exercise leaderlike initiative and responsibility, using their local knowledge to assess problems at their level and move to solve them.

To emphasize the need for dispersed leadership does not deny the need for extremely able top leadership. We need our great high-level leaders. But they will be more effective in every way if the systems over which they preside are made vital by dispersed leadership. We must demand high performance at every level of the society.

PARTICIPATION

It is my belief, widely shared today, that leaders should have a nurturing relationship to their constituency, should empower their followers, should enable group members to achieve goals of the members' own choosing. But I do not believe that constituencies should sit around waiting for such nice things to happen. And that brings us to the subject of participation.

Participation takes many forms. The first duties of citizens are not of a sophisticated political nature. Those duties are to look after one another in the family circle, get themselves educated and equipped to support themselves, obey the law, pay their taxes and rear their children as responsible members of the community. These are authentic forms of participation, though they are rarely mentioned in discussions of the subject.

The word *participation* has been used in recent decades chiefly to denote political involvement, as in the phrase "participatory democracy." But it is not wise to allow a valuable word to be so arbitrarily narrowed. Parents who serve on the school board are participating. So is the senior citizen who serves as a volunteer in a hospice for the terminally ill. So is the college student who serves as a volunteer tutor for disadvantaged children. All are making their constructive contribution to the life of the community—taking part, participating. The voluntary sector of our society offers endless opportunities for such involvement.

But in the discussion that follows I shall focus on citizen action in the political realm. In the political arena we ask that citizens follow public affairs intelligently and vote. Beyond that many people will give no time to political responsibilities, some because they are unmotivated, others because they have deep commitments in directions other than public affairs (to their families, their jobs, their churches).

But others—many others—choose to go further, participating in the politically active sense of the word. For citizens to participate actively in the workings of their society is not only good democratic doctrine, it is essential to the renewal of the society. Communication upward from grassroots to higher levels of decision regenerates the society.

Citizens should give at least part of their attention to the public interest as they understand it—the interest of the total community, state, nation, or planet. This is not to say that they should ignore self-interest: our polity expects and requires that individuals and groups speak out vigorously on their own particular concerns. But the voices of special interest groups are on the whole well represented in the national chorus. There are rarely enough individuals speaking out for what they conceive to be the public interest.

CITIZEN ORGANIZATIONS

If individuals wish to be active in public affairs beyond the voting booth, they must consider the usefulness of affiliation with one or another citizen group. To speak out is one thing, to be listened to is quite another. Our fondness for individualism draws us to the lone crusader, but most successful citizen action is group action. Fortunately, thanks to the measureless fertility of our society in spawning voluntary groups, there is an organization to suit virtually every interest.

Some of the citizen action—or community action—groups are local, some national. National groups are usually necessary if the purpose is to accomplish nationwide results, since the instrument of final action is very likely to be the Congress of the United States. Even when a local group's aims are strictly local, it may be that those aims will be more surely achieved if the nation as a whole is aware of the issues and concerned about them. For that reason, most local groups will want to have links to one or another national organization.

Yet there is enormous value to grassroots organizations in which citizens can work with their neighbors under leadership that is drawn from their own ranks, and can see with their own eyes the launching of a citizen effort and the local outcome of the effort.

One of the interesting developments of the past two decades is the emergence in low-income areas of grassroots community organizations that work on housing, economic development, job training, day care and the like. Some community development organizations finance and operate shopping centers, industrial parks and even small factories.

The Mississippi Action for Community Education (MACE), together with its sister organization, the Delta Foundation, has operated in the two-hundred-mile stretch of poverty-stricken countryside bordering the Mississippi south of Memphis. Illiteracy, inadequate health care, unemployment, substandard housing and lack of sewer and water systems plagued the area. The two organizations have engaged in an extraordinary variety of activities including job training, education reform, leadership development, voter registration, and the creation of local community institutions. They have operated a revolving loan fund and provided technical assistance for small entrepreneurs, owned several small factories, built housing for the elderly and the handicapped, supported farm cooperatives and community-owned supermarkets.

Larry Farmer, president of MACE, says, "Jobs, income, decent living conditions—these should not really entail genius. They just require determination and the belief that it can be done."[1]

SHARING LEADERSHIP TASKS

Forty years ago Kenneth Benne and Paul Sheats saw the leadership role "in terms of functions to be performed within a group in helping the group to grow and to work productively." They pointed out that groups may operate with various degrees of diffusion of leadership functions among members or with concentration of such functions in one member or a few members.[2]

Alex Bavelas expressed somewhat similar thoughts in 1960[3] and more recently Edgar H. Schein, in his valuable book *Organizational Psychology*,[4] wrote: "Leadership is best thought of as a function within the organization. . . . It can be distributed among the members of a group . . . and is not automatically vested in . . . whoever has formal authority. Good leadership and good membership, therefore, blend into each other . . . in an effective organization. It is just as much the task of a member to help the group reach its goals as it is the task of the formal leader."

It is interesting to reflect on why such a significant insight, expressed so clearly by authoritative voices a generation apart, has been so neglected in contemporary leadership literature. Leadership is rarely discussed as a set of functions, and virtually never as functions that might be diffused among the group. Yet those are the realities.

Most of the endlessly debated questions about leadership are ancient, but there is one that has a distinctly modern ring: *How can we define the role of leaders in the way that most effectively releases the creative energies of followers in the pursuit of shared purposes?* The concept of sharing leadership tasks responds to that question.

The democratic impulse—the desire of people in general to have a hand in the affairs of their community or state—emerged some twenty-five centuries ago. At first it focused on participation in choosing those who made the community's decisions, and participation in the decisions themselves. It was the "deciding" function that mattered most, and the focus was on government.

Today, for proponents of participatory or populist democracy, the focus is still on the deciding function as it relates to governing, and the preferred mode is for citizens to decide after face-to-face discussion of issues in town-meeting-like forums. That is a worthy focus, but I have something broader in mind. The leadership tasks involved in keeping a community going are richly varied and extend far beyond the deciding function. We must find a way of thinking which reflects that variety, and the concept of sharing leadership tasks does just that.

How Sharing Occurs

It may be helpful to cite some examples.

On any athletic team that is falling behind in a contest there are always a few individuals who undertake on their own to prevent a drop in morale by building the confidence of their teammates. They are sharing the leadership task of motivating.

When a group is internally divided over some issues, there are always a few who, acting in a wholly unofficial capacity, try to heal the rift. They are sharing the leadership task of unifying.

When an organization is clinging to outmoded ways that no longer get results there are always a few clearheaded and courageous individuals who speak out for modernization. They are sharing the leadership task of renewing.

In the mid-1960s Erik Jonsson, mayor of Dallas, invited a large number of citizens to play active roles in helping to set goals for their city, and many hundreds accepted the invitation.

What I have called "leadership tasks" are functions that, if properly performed, enable the group to get on with its purposes. The sharing of these tasks by group members is not a dream of something that might be made to happen; it is something that is already happening, has no doubt always happened—and could be made to happen on a larger scale.

Advantage of Sharing Leadership Tasks

The only hope for vitality in a large-scale organization is the willingness of a great many people scattered throughout the organization to take the initiative in identifying problems and solving them. Without that, the organization becomes another of those sodden, inert, nonadaptive bureaucracies that are the bane of modern corporate and governmental life—rigid, unimaginative and totally unequipped to deal with a swiftly changing environment.

Passivity is only one of the root problems of large-scale, complex communities and organizations. An almost equally difficult problem is specialization and the fragmentation of a community or enterprise into segments that are not always in touch with one another, and not committed to shared goals. At a moment of crisis a mayor once said to me, "Every group in this town is pushing zealously for its own special interest. I sometimes think I'm the only one around who worries about the future of the whole city." Having spent two of the most active years of my life working with mayors on urban problems, I know how he felt, but my experience did not bear out his complaint. I found many citizens ready and eager to share the task of thinking about the future of their city, even willing to expend considerable energy to solve its problems.

The taking of responsibility is at the heart of leadership. To the extent that leadership tasks are shared, responsibility is shared.

The wider sharing of leadership tasks could sharply lower the barriers to leadership. For every person now leading there could be many who share leadership tasks, testing their skills, enjoying the lift of spirit that comes with assuming responsibility, and putting their feet on the lower rungs of a ladder that rises to higher leadership responsibilities. Many who lack the self-assurance to think of themselves as leaders would find within themselves the confidence to test the lower rungs of the ladder. Others who now feel excluded, shut out from the possibility of leadership, would find that the entry points were numerous and welcoming.

ACCOUNTABILITY

The sharing of leadership tasks offers challenging opportunities to citizens, but citizens have another and sterner duty with respect to leadership: They must hold leaders to account.

One means of protecting ourselves from exploitation by leaders is to deprive them of power. To a degree we have done that and will continue to do it, but the strategy has its limits. At the same time that we diminish the power of leaders, we are forever calling for leaders "who can get the job done." For the society to get its work done, leaders and the systems over which they preside must be granted some measure of power. It is a common experience for leaders today to have far less power than they need to accomplish the tasks we hand them. They must have the power to get results. *But those who are granted power must be held accountable.*

Not just leaders but powerholders in general must be held accountable. It is a hard fact that most of the people whose actions affect our lives are powerholders rather than leaders. An entrenched bureaucrat utterly unknown to the public can profoundly affect public policy. In the economic sphere, a land developer, a specialist in corporate takeovers, a gifted marketer, a greedy banker may affect the course of events and the lives of a great many people without the slightest pretense of leadership.

Much of the law is an attempt to set limits on one or another category of powerholder, and one of the uses of leaders is that, as visible and presumably accountable persons, they can be called upon to keep less visible powerholders within reasonable bounds.

Broadly speaking the goal is to hold power accountable in all spheres of life, but the primary focus must be on government since a properly functioning government can help hold power accountable in the rest of society. We can never make government wholly efficient or pure. But we can go far toward making it accessible, responsive and accountable, giving a measure of reality to that universally quoted, sporadically honored phrase, "the consent of the governed."

Systems That Ensure Accountability

It comes down to the task of designing the system in such a way as to *ensure* accountability. Our eighteenth-century leaders liked the admonition "Eternal vigilance is the price of liberty," but it turns out that free citizens are not eternally vigilant. They keep dozing off; and on one or another front their liberties are infringed upon. If they are lucky, they wake up and combat the threat to their liberties before it is too late. But if success attends their efforts, they promptly doze off again. Citizens must make the most of the moments of wakefulness to build (or rebuild) sleepless monitoring systems—a free press, an uncorrupted judiciary, citizen advocacy groups and the like—that warn of the erosion of liberty and the abuse of power.

We would be well advised to assume that those in power will overreach and abuse power sooner or later if the system permits it. Thomas Jefferson said, "In questions of power . . . let us hear no more of confidence in man, but bind him down from mischief by the chains of the Constitution."

The necessary protections begin with the rule of law and our constitutional system. Our arrangements for dispersing power play a crucial role, as do the provisions we have made for an educated citizenry. The guarantees of free speech and the enforcement of statutes protecting civil liberties are fundamental.

Equally important is the existence of well-established modes of citizen participation. The prime instrument of political accountability is the electoral process, so it must be protected with jealous concern. That means removing obstacles to voter registration, getting out the vote, ensuring an open nominating process and guarding the integrity of elections.

The gravest threat to the integrity of the electoral process today is the capacity of money to buy political outcomes. As the influence of money increases, the lawmakers' link of accountability to the electorate becomes relatively weaker than the links to big donors.

It is desirable that the political parties be open to rank-and-file participation, that there be citizen access to litigation to correct government excesses or inaction, and that other procedures for the redress of grievances be readily available.

Openness is a necessary condition. Citizens cannot give "the consent of the governed" if they do not know what is going on. Hence the importance of statutes providing for open meetings where feasible, disclosures bearing on conflict of interest, and freedom of information. It is a universal characteristic of human systems, governmental or not, that those running the system will, over time, devise ways of keeping "inside information" inside. Over years, governing bodies design institutional arrangements that make it difficult for citizens to obtain the information necessary to independent judgment. There is of course in any government agency a small body of information that should not be divulged for reasons of security or invasion of privacy, but the agency's natural impulse will be to withhold information far beyond that perimeter.

Citizen action beyond the ballot is essential if government is to be held to account. When citizens walk away from the polling booth imagining that they have done their whole duty, they deceive themselves. Politics is a game that goes on with undiminished zest after the crowds have left the stadium. All of the special interests that influence government have found ways of "voting between." Citizen action is not only good for government, it is good for the citizens doing the acting. And good constituents tend to produce good leaders.

The Independent Sector

John W. Gardner spent nineteen years working for the Carnegie Corporation, a grantmaking foundation, two years with the Urban Coalition working on the problems of the cities, and seven years with Common Cause, a nonprofit citizens' organization. His knowledge of nonprofit organizations and agendas, coupled with an awareness of their importance as the home of "civil society" and the chief arena for the formation of social capital, led him to join with Brian O'Connell in founding INDEPENDENT SECTOR in 1980. Today, INDEPENDENT SECTOR is a large and active organization serving as a forum for the widely diverse groups that make up the nonprofit sector—churches, schools, hospitals, foundations, symphonies, social clubs, shelters, neighborhood associations, and many more. The goals of the organization are to enable the disparate segments of the sector to be in effective communication with one another, to stimulate research and improve management within the sector, and to foster public education on its role.

In a totalitarian state, most organized activity is governmental—and the little that is not is heavily controlled or influenced by government. Almost everything is bureaucratized and subject to central goal setting and rule making.

In the nations that the world thinks of as democracies, there is, in contrast, a large area of activity outside of government. The United States probably outstrips all others in the size and autonomy of its nongovernmental sector. The major portion of our private sector consists of activities designed for profit; a smaller portion consists of nonprofit activities. Both profit and nonprofit segments have many dealings with government, but both recognize that their vitality depends in part on their success in holding themselves free of central bureaucratic definition of goals.

The nonprofit segment has been variously labeled the voluntary sector, the third sector or—more recently—the independent sector. In its diversity and strength it is uniquely American—not in the fact of its existence, because it exists elsewhere, but in its extraordinary richness and variety. It encompasses a remarkable army of American institutions—libraries, museums, religious organizations, schools and colleges, organizations concerned with health and welfare, citizen action groups, neighborhood organizations and countless other groups such as Alcoholics Anonymous, the Urban League, the 4H Clubs, the Women's Political Caucus, the Salvation Army, and the United Way.

The independent—or nonprofit—sector is a part of American life in which you are allowed to pursue truth, even if you're going in the wrong direction, allowed to experiment even if you're bound to fail, to map unknown territory even if you get lost; a sector in which we may strive to alleviate misery and redress grievances, to give rein to the mind's curiosity and the soul's longing, to seek beauty where we can and defend truth where we must, to combat the ancient impulse to hate and fear the tribe in the next valley, to find cures and console the incurable, to prepare for tomorrow's crisis and preserve yesterday's wisdom, and to pursue the questions others won't pursue because they're too busy or lazy or fearful or jaded. It's a sector for seed planting and pathfinding, for lost causes and for causes that yet may win, and in the words of George Bernard Shaw, "for the future and the past, for the posterity that has no vote and the tradition that never had any . . . for the eternal against the expedient, for the evolutionary appetite against the day's gluttony, for intellectual integrity, for humanity."

—Speech to INDEPENDENT SECTOR membership, Washington, D.C., 1983

Living, Leading, and the American Dream

When people are left free to pursue all kinds of activities, as they are in this country, a surprising number will choose to serve some community purpose. The private pursuit of public purpose is an honored tradition in American life. Americans do not regard the furtherance of public purpose as a monopoly of government, and that belief has brought a great release of human energy.

Given the level of human commitment, one then needs another, more earthy ingredient—money. So it turns out that most of the activities of the nonprofit sector depend an another powerful American tradition—the tradition of private giving for public purposes. The ingredient of private giving supplies the element of freedom.

In the few foreign countries where there is any considerable private philanthropy, it is usually traceable to a few wealthy people. Only in the United States are the gifts of the wealthy simply the peak of a pyramid with a very, very broad base—a base of modest contributions made by millions of individuals. Few Americans realize how broad that base really is. For the most part private giving in this country is a Mississippi River of small gifts.

Government tax policy has deliberately fostered our tradition of giving. The tax deductibility of charitable gifts is a long-established means of furthering an authentically American idea—that it is a good thing for a great many people in their capacity as private citizens to contribute to charitable, religious, scientific and educational activities of their choice. We have demonstrated that preserving a role for the private citizen in these matters encourages individual involvement and keeps alive the sense of personal caring and concern that is so essential if a mass society is to retain an element of humaneness.

The area of our national life encompassed by the charitable tax deduction lies at the very heart of our intellectual and spiritual strivings, at the very heart of our feeling about one another and about our life as a people. Traditionally, government leaders have agreed that here, if anywhere, government should keep its distance and honor the maximum degree of independence; here, if anywhere, the personal, family, and community spirit should be preserved; here, if anywhere, those elements of the human mind and spirit that wither under bureaucratization should have a place to stand free.

In 1969 I was chairman of the National Urban Coalition, which was coping with the problems of poverty and race underlying the devastating urban riots of the late sixties. One day I received a letter signed by ten enlisted men stationed at Ford Ord, California, and training for service in Vietnam. They expressed deep concern for the urban problems I was working on—and they had a suggestion. They said: "We propose that during the next decade we reallocate (through private giving) $20–$50 billion of our personal income into programs of social reform to supplement whatever the Federal government is willing to finance . . . statistically if one-tenth of the people in the country could be persuaded to tithe 10 percent of their income after taxes for a period of ten years, then $50 billion could be raised."

Their numbers weren't quite right, but that's not the point. The astonishing thing is that attached to their letter were ten personal checks representing in each case 10 percent of the individual's enlisted pay for the preceding month. I sat for a long time staring at the checks. These young men who were headed into battle still had time to think rationally and constructively about their country's dilemmas. They saw a problem. They believed it was their responsibility to worry about a solution. And they took action.

All work came to a halt in our offices as everyone read the letter and looked at the checks. One young woman whose husband was in Vietnam burst into tears.

I tell the story to illustrate a truth that all of you know very well—that splendid gifts such as those of Andrew Carnegie, John D. Rockefeller and others are only a modest part of the story of American philanthropy.

—Speech to Council on Foundations, New York City, 1997

The policy has worked. It has permitted the emergence of great world centers of learning; it has made our museums and medical centers famous throughout the world; and it has nourished an enormous variety of neighborhood and community activities.

Have there been abuses? Of course. But they have been trivial compared to the great and lasting benefits in preserving our free society.

ATTRIBUTES OF THE SECTOR

It is worth reviewing some of the characteristics of the independent sector that make it a powerfully positive force in American life. There is no point in comparing it favorably or unfavorably with other sectors of the society. Each has its function.

Perhaps the most striking feature of the sector is its relative freedom from constraints and its resulting pluralism. Within the bounds of the law, all kinds of people can pursue any idea or program they wish. Unlike government, an independent sector group need not ascertain that its idea or philosophy is supported by some large constituency, and unlike the business sector, it does not need to pursue only those ideas which will be profitable. If a handful of people want to back a new idea, they need seek no larger consensus.

Americans have always believed in pluralism—the idea that a free nation should be hospitable to many sources of initiative, many kinds of institutions, many conflicting beliefs, and many competing economic units. Our pluralism allows individuals and groups to pursue goals that they themselves formulate, and out of that pluralism has come virtually all of our creativity.

Not every institution in the independent sector is innovative, but the sector provides a hospitable environment for innovation. Ideas for doing things in a different, and possibly better, way spring up constantly. If they do not fill a need, they quickly fall by the wayside. What remain are the few ideas and innovations that have long-term value. New ideas and new ways of doing things test the validity of accepted practice and build an inventory of possible alternative solutions which can be used if circumstances change.

Government bureaucracies are simply not constructed to permit the emergence of countless new ideas, and even less suited to the winnowing out of bad ideas. An idea that is controversial, unpopular, or strange has little chance in either the commercial or the political marketplace. In the nonprofit sector, someone with a new idea or program may very well find the few followers necessary to help nurse it to maturity. Virtually every significant social idea of the past century in this country has been nurtured in the nonprofit sector.

The sector is the natural home of nonmajoritarian impulses, movements, and values. It comfortably harbors innovators, maverick movements, groups that feel they must fight for their place in the sun, and critics of both liberal and conservative persuasion.

Institutions of the nonprofit sector are in a position to serve as the guardians of intellectual and artistic freedom. Both the commercial and political marketplaces are subject to leveling forces that may threaten standards of excellence. In the nonprofit sector, the fiercest champions of excellence may have their say. So may the champions of liberty and justice.

The sector preserves individual initiative and responsibility. As in the for-profit sector, there are innumerable opportunities for the resourceful— to initiate, explore, grow, cooperate, lead, make a difference. At a time in history when individuality is threatened by the impersonality of large-scale social organization, the sector's emphasis on individual initiative is a priceless counterweight.

To deal effectively with the ailments of our society today, individual initiative isn't enough, there has to be some way of linking the individual with the community. In the independent sector, such linkages are easily forged. Citizens banding together can tackle a small neighborhood problem or a great national issue.

The past century has seen a more or less steady deterioration of American communities as coherent entities with the morale and binding values that hold people together. Our sense of community has been badly battered, and every social philosopher emphasizes the need to restore it. What is at stake is the individual's sense of responsibility for something beyond the self. A spirit of concern for one's fellows is virtually impossible to sustain in a vast, impersonal, featureless society. Only in coherent human groupings (the neighborhood, the family, the community) can we keep alive our shared values and preserve the simple human awareness that we need one another. We must recreate a society that has its social and spiritual roots firmly planted in such groupings—so firmly planted that those roots cannot be ripped out by the winds of change, nor by the dehumanizing, automatizing forces of the contemporary world.

This is not to express a sentimental aversion to large-scale organization or national action. Many of the forces acting upon us can only be dealt with by large-scale organizations, national in scope, including a vigorous government. But if we intend that the overarching governmental organizations we create be our servants and not our masters, we must have vital communities.

THE GREAT SHARED TASK

My observations about the positive aspects of the sector are not intended to gloss over the flaws evident in its institutions and organizations. Some nonprofit institutions are far gone in decay. Some are so badly managed as to make a mockery of every good intention they might have had. There is fraud, mediocrity, and silliness. In short, the human and institutional failures that afflict government and business are also present in the voluntary sector. Beyond that, it is the essence of pluralism (in the society as a whole as well as in the sector) that no particular observer will approve of everything that goes on. If you can't find a nonprofit institution that you can honestly disrespect, then something has gone wrong with our pluralism.

But these considerations are trivial compared to the attributes that make the independent sector a source of deep and positive meaning in our national life. If it were to disappear from our national life, we would be less distinctly American. The sector enhances our creativity, enlivens our communities, nurtures individual responsibility, stirs life at the grass roots, and reminds us that we were born free. Its vitality is rooted in good soil—civic pride, compassion, a philanthropic tradition, a strong problem-solving impulse, a sense of individual responsibility and, despite what cynics may say, an irrepressible commitment to the great shared task of improving our life together.

The American Dream

This essay was written in 1976, the year of the Bicentennial. It was published in the IBM publication *THINK Magazine*.

There was—there is—an American Dream. A dozen honest, perceptive observers would each sketch it differently. But why not? It is variegated, characterized by strong themes and subtle contradictions, things of the mind and things of the heart, continuity and evolution, a sense of place, symbols, a history, shared memories. It's alive, and living things change. What follows is one observer's sketch of a rich subject.

There have been, of course, as many American dreams as there have been Americans who dreamed. Dreams of freedom and dreams of material comfort, dreams of brotherhood and dreams of greed, dreams of success and dreams of escape. The list is endless. That list itemized is not the American Dream.

The word *dream* in the sense of something desirable that might come to pass implies effortlessness and pleasure. The American Dream bears no resemblance to that. It has required great exertions, stamina and hard work in the heat of the day. It has brought exhilaration and pleasure but also suffering and hardship.

The Dream began in England and Europe, in the minds of individuals. The fantasies of empire that moved the colonizing nations and trading companies were never the American Dream. The Dream began as individual dreams of opportunity—all kinds of opportunity. For many it was the opportunity to pursue their religion without harassment; for others it was the opportunity to escape, to be free, to better their lot, to get rich, to start again, to find excitement.

Then, early in the life of the colonies, a distinctive way of thinking about society began to emerge. Despite great regional differences in style, the colonists developed some strikingly similar attitudes. Without attempting a complete list, one might mention an unwillingness to import to these shores the class structure and political patterns of Europe, a pattern of industriousness and self-reliance born of necessity, a restless habit of "moving on," a distinct taste for risk taking (in founding new colonies, in religious dissent, in land speculation), and an abiding distaste for hierarchy.

Before the 1600s came to an end, ways of thinking had emerged that made the Revolution inevitable. The new society wasn't born in 1776. That's when it was old enough to leave home.

In the last decades of the eighteenth century, crucial ingredients of the American Dream were put into words—not just the words in the founding documents, but words spoken in meeting halls and written in memoirs. The words said that we—as a nation—were going to make liberty and justice a reality. We asserted that "All men are created equal." We were going to honor universal "rights of man." We were going to set an example of enlightenment to the world.

It was all incredibly buoyant, vital, young and prideful—and only the wisest of our Founding Fathers caught a glimpse of the enormous difficulties and challenges woven into the Dream. To our youthful nation, a sense of mission came as naturally as a leap in the spring sunshine.

All of our history since then has been one long instruction in the difficulties of the Dream. We know now—all too well—that our Founding Fathers didn't hand us a completed task. We have had to work—still have to work—very hard to make real the ideals expressed in the founding documents.

It isn't possible to separate the Dream from the people who dreamed. Most of the colonists and later immigrants came on their own initiative and were perhaps in their very nature more venturesome than those who

Living, Leading, and the American Dream

remained behind. But some of their attributes can only be explained by the experience on these shores, attributes that came somehow out of the vast land, out of the endless, bustling movement, out of our escape from the burden of history. There was buoyancy, a sense of the future, a taste for improvisation, confidence, a passion for self-improvement, a resilient willingness to keep trying. (Later we came to love success, but that was never what America was about: America was about *trying*—and the opportunity to try.)

As the years passed, the Dream took on deeper, richer, more mature tones. We experienced failure and tragedy. We learned that we were imperfect. We learned that the world was complicated, and that we ourselves were complicated.

At the same time, with every decade that passed, the Dream was given texture by an ever-deeper sense of our land and our past. Compared with Europeans, Americans were irreverent toward tradition. Yet slowly—deeper than words—the images, symbols and memories accumulated: Valley Forge, the frontier, the wide Missouri, the gold rush, Civil War battlefields, the face of Lincoln, sod houses on the prairie, the Little Big Horn, Ellis Island, immigrant neighborhoods, the American Expeditionary Force, the Model T, bread lines, Pearl Harbor, the affluent society, civil rights, Vietnam. Good memories and heartbreaking memories. Growth and tragedy. Lessons learned and lessons still to learn.

A few of the lessons were so bitter that some observers feared we'd never recover. And, ironically, the dozen years preceding our two hundredth birthday were particularly troubled years: assassinations, bitter racial conflict, a hated war and one of the greatest scandals in our political history.

Americans today are not unmarked by those troubled years. There is uncertainty. There is contempt for much that has been pretentious and false in our national life. But anyone who looks closely will see something else: resilience, stamina, the courage to look at our faults—and under all the noisy, strife-ridden, often self-indulgent surface of our national life, an insistent desire to do better.

We tend to imagine that earlier generations had more "character"; but one must render a mixed judgment. Nineteenth- and early twentieth-century

Americans had an essentially youthful notion that nothing could really go wrong for America: every problem would be solved. The Americans in every walk of life today—teachers, businesspeople, workers, professionals and civil servants—who are seriously tackling the problems we face as a nation are, in important ways, more mature. They take a hardier view of life. They know there isn't a solution to every problem. They know there are no Utopias, that society is not perfectible nor can humankind be made perfect. They know that America's fate is inextricably linked to the fate of the human species and the planet Earth. They have a new hard-bitten morale that enables them to face those discouraging truths and still strive with every ounce of their energy to prevail. And that new hard-bitten morale can be the saving of this nation.

Our Founding Fathers knew that humans were flawed and that therefore human societies would be flawed. But the soaring optimism of nineteenth-century America left their wisdom behind. In our attitudes today we are closer to the nation's founders than were the Americans of a century ago. Our sense of mission has been chastened and purged of the pride that goes before a fall.

And we haven't given up. True, there is hypocrisy, self-indulgence and cynicism; and we have our share of rascals and fools. But with respect to most Americans, scratch the surface and you'll find a yearning for something better. We want to be better people. We want to help make this a better country in a better world. We want our liberty, so that we can continue to work on our problems as a free people. We want justice for everyone— and we know now that some of the obstacles to achieving it are in our own hearts and minds. We still treasure the idea of opportunity—to be what each of us can be as individuals, to be what we can be as a nation.

And we want more down-to-earth things too: a decent life for our kids, a job, respect, dignity in our later years. Most of us know that we've got to work for those things. An endless stream of news stories leaves the impression that America is awash with people who are dangerously irresponsible. But most Americans work hard, raise their kids, love their country, stretch each dollar, mourn their dead, and keep going.

There have been enormous changes in America since the beginning. No doubt there are great changes ahead—in patterns of work, political and economic arrangements, the shape of familiar institutions. The American reality will never be static. Nor will the Dream: like all things in the realm of values, it will be re-created in each generation by caring men and women. It will guide them, and they in turn will keep it alive by reshaping it to meet the unrolling future.

A great many Americans are doing just that today by working seriously on the problems we face as a nation, as a species, as a planet: problems of peace and of commerce, of social justice and of productivity, of teaching and learning. I salute them. Looking back, I have great affection for the morning optimism of a younger nation. But my deepest admiration goes to those many Americans who are keeping the Dream alive today.

$\boxed{21}$

Freedom and Obligation, Liberty and Duty

In his first book, *Excellence,* John W. Gardner set down themes that would appear again and again in his writings and speeches in subsequent years. These were the themes of his lifetime: America, Freedom, Obligations, Family, Excellence. One hears the echoes of this first iteration throughout his work, and most particularly in "The American Dream," written in the year of the Bicentennial, and "The American Experiment," written near the end of his life. The tasks for Americans changed little as the challenges were ever changing.

More than two centuries ago the founders of this nation set out to show the world that free citizens could build a great civilization. They knew that the world was watching them and they had sublime confidence that they were going to show the world something worth watching. Today you may survey vast stretches of contemporary life without detecting any sign that Americans remember that high goal. Our founders knew that in a world largely hostile to the idea of freedom, as the world was then and is now, a free society would have to prove that it is capable of—and worthy of—survival. The requirement is unchanged today. Free societies must prove their ability to make good on their promises and to keep alive their cherished values. And more than that, they must prove their vigor, their capacity to practice the disciplined virtues, their capacity to achieve excellence.

The free society is still the exceptional society: the ideal is still unattainable or unacceptable to most of the world's peoples. Many live under governments that have no inclination to foster freedom. Others are hemmed in by their own backwardness, or by rigid social stratification. The foes of freedom are still ready to argue that the unruliness, greed, and self-indulgence of human beings make a free society simply impractical.

It is hard for Americans to realize that the survival of the idea for which this nation stands is not inevitable. It may survive if enough Americans care enough. Part of the problem is that many individuals today no longer have a compelling feeling for the mutual dependence of the individual and the group, meaning by *group* the family, community, and nation.

The family and community have much to give the individual: nurture in infancy, the release of potentialities through education, the protection of individual rights, a sense of identity and belonging. In return, the individual must pay tithes of allegiance—must give something back—to family, community, nation, humankind.

We're free within a framework of obligations to our family, to our community, to the nation—and, of course, depending upon our beliefs, obligations to our God and to our conception of an ethical order.

We must freely grant our allegiance to the society that gives us freedom. Montesquieu said a republic can survive only as long as its citizens love it. Freedom and obligation, liberty and duty—that's the deal. May we never forget it. May we never deceive ourselves. It isn't in the grand design that we can have freedom without obligation. Not for long.

REAFFIRMATION

I believe that most Americans would welcome a new burst of commitment. I do not believe the self-centeredness and disengagement of which they are accused is their natural state. *The best-kept secret in America today is that people would rather work hard for something they believe in than live a life of aimless diversion.*

Ask retired persons whether they would trade their leisure for activity in which they could apply their full powers toward something they believed in. The religious precept that you must lose yourself to find yourself is no less true at the secular level. No one who has observed devoted scientists in their laboratories can doubt the spiritual rewards of such work. The same is true of all who are working toward goals that represent the highest values of their society.

Of course, we all have a certain skepticism about the expenditure of effort beyond that required by the exigencies of the system. What's in it for me? It is a question born of deep habituation to the marketing of one's energies in return for the necessities of life. But we are talking now about another kind of arena and another kind of transaction. And this transaction is not subject to the same peasant craftiness. Quite the reverse. The more one gives, the more one gets.

We fall into the error of thinking that happiness necessarily involves ease, diversion, tranquillity—a state in which all of one's wishes are satisfied. For most people, happiness is not to be found in this vegetative state but in striving toward meaningful goals. For dedicated men and women life is the endless pursuit of goals, some of them unattainable. Such people may often be tense, worried, fatigued. They may have little of the leisure one associates with the storybook conception of happiness. But the truth is that happiness in the sense of total gratification is not a state to which humans can aspire. It is for the cows, possibly for the birds, but not for us.

Of course, every line of behavior has its pathology, and there is a pathology of dedication. People sometimes commit themselves to vicious goals; or their commitment to worthy goals becomes so fanatical that they destroy as much as they create. And there are the "true believers" who surrender themselves to a mass movement or to dogmatic beliefs to escape the responsibilities of freedom. But a free society wants only one kind of devotion, the devotion of free, rational, responsible individuals.

SHARED PURPOSES

A free people, precisely because they prize individuality, must take special pains to ensure that their shared purposes do not disintegrate. No society will successfully resolve its internal conflicts if its only asset is cleverness in the management of these conflicts. It must also have compelling goals that are shared by the conflicting parties, and it must have a sense of movement toward these goals. The conflicting elements must have a vision that lifts their minds and spirits above the tensions of the moment.

It is not entirely easy to suggest a list of aims on which Americans would agree; but that is as it should be. We do not want or expect Americans to come to full agreement on a standard list of goals. We expect individual Americans to set their own priorities, not only in their personal lives but in matters affecting the common good. The result is diversity of values, diversity of opinion, diversity of aims. But most Americans are not really in doubt about the more serious of our shared aims. We know what they are. *We know that they are difficult. And we know that we have not achieved them.*

Are examples needed?

We want peace with justice. We want a world that doesn't live in fear of the bomb, a world that acknowledges the rule of law, a world in which no nation can play bully and no nation need live in fear. How many Americans would disagree with that purpose? Is it easy? Have we achieved it? Read your morning paper.

We want freedom. We don't think the individual was born to have someone else's foot on his neck—or someone else's hand over his mouth. We want freedom at home and we want a world in which freedom is possible. Who would disagree with that as a national aim? Who would call it easy? Who would say we've achieved it?

We believe in the dignity and worth of the individual and it is our unshakable purpose to protect and preserve that dignity.

We believe that men and women should be enabled to achieve the best that is in them, and we are the declared enemies of all conditions, such as disease, ignorance, or poverty, that stunt the individual and prevent such fulfillment.

We believe in equality of all our citizens, regardless of race, gender, or religion, with respect to the rights specified in the Constitution.

Will there be arguments as to *how* to achieve these goals? Of course. Are there dissidents who don't believe in one or another of these goals—or any of them, for that matter? Of course.

These items do not exhaust the list. But they are enough to demonstrate the possibility of formulating aims on which large numbers of Americans can agree.

A list of national purposes cannot—and should not—include all of the things that individuals in the society cherish. Our kind of society gives ample scope to aims that are essentially individual in nature—such as devotion to loved ones and to religious purposes.

Although we have been talking about the secular aims of the society, most of these aims have roots in our religious tradition. The religious substratum in American life runs deep and has marked us indelibly as a people. Some of the aims we have listed were conceived and brought to flower in a religious tradition. Others, though not religious in origin, have drawn powerful nourishment from religious groups and individuals. To state the matter in general terms, there is bound to be an intimate connection between the individual's attitude toward these aims and those deeper dealings with "the universal and eternal" that we call religion.

WE NEED OUR YOUNG PEOPLE

Perhaps nothing is more effective in suppressing any spirit of public endeavor on the part of the individual than the overpowering size and complexity of the joint enterprise in which we are supposed to be participants. The tasks facing our ancestors may have been grim and often frightening, but generally they were also obvious. Each person knew what he or she must do. But what does the individual do about inflation, about international organization, about the balance of trade? Individual Americans—busy earning a living, repapering the dining room, getting the children off to school, and paying the bills—don't hear one clear call to action. They hear a jumble of outcries and alarms, of fanfares and dirges, of voices crying "Hurry!" and voices crying "Wait!" Meanwhile they have problems of their own.

If it is confusing to adults, it is even more so for young people. How can they believe that they are even needed? Surely only great organizations can cope with such a giant system. If there is a problem, surely highly coordinated teams of experts must be studying it. If there are cracks in the world, learned specialists must be measuring them.

In short, complexity seems to be the universal condition, organization the universal requirement. What can the individual do? It is not surprising that young people shrug their shoulders and find something else to talk about.

This is disturbing when one recognizes the exhilarating effect of being needed and responding to that need—whether the need is within one's family, one's community, one's nation, or humankind. There is danger in a conviction on the part of young people that they are not needed by their own community. "The sense of uselessness," said Thomas Huxley, "is the severest shock which our system can sustain."[1]

But we do need our young people—desperately. Why not tell them we need every bit of help we can get? As Whitehead said, "We must produce a great age, or see the collapse of the upward striving of our race."[2]

One thing we might tell them—at the same time that we're telling ourselves—is this: "If you believe in a free society, be worthy of a free society." Every good man or woman strengthens society. In this day of sophisticated judgments on such matters, that is a notably unfashionable thing to say, but it is true. Men and women of integrity, by their very existence, rekindle the belief that as a people we can live above the level of moral squalor. We need that belief; a cynical community is a corrupt community.

More than any other form of government, democracy requires a certain faith in human possibilities. The best argument for democracy is the existence of men and women who justify that faith. It follows that one of the best ways to serve democracy is to be that kind of person.

Living, Leading, and the American Dream

THE PURSUIT OF EXCELLENCE

When we raise our sights, strive for excellence, dedicate ourselves to the highest goals of our society, we are enrolling in an ancient and meaningful cause—the agelong struggle of humans to realize the best that is in them. Humans reaching toward the most exalted goals they can conceive, striving impatiently and restlessly for excellence, have achieved religious insights, created works of art, penetrated secrets of the universe and set standards of conduct that heighten our sense of pride—and dignity as human beings. William Hazlitt said, "Man is the only animal that laughs and weeps; for he is the only animal that is struck with the difference between what things are and what they ought to be."[3] On the other hand, humans without standards, with their eyes on the ground, have proved over and over again, in every society and at every period of history—including the present—that they can be lower than the beasts, morally and ethically blind, living a life devoid of meaning. A concern for excellence, a devotion to standards, a respect for the human mind and spirit at its best move us toward the former condition and away from the latter. C.G.J. Jacobi, when asked why he devoted himself to mathematics, said, *"Pour l'honneur de l'esprit humain."*

We must face the fact that there are a good many things in our character and in our national life that are inimical to standards—shallowness, complacency, the pursuit of a fast buck, a fondness for shortcuts, a willingness to tolerate incompetence, to name only a few.

The importance of competence as a condition of freedom has been widely ignored (as some newly independent nations have found to their sorrow). An amiable fondness for the graces of a free society is not enough. Keeping a free society free and vital and strong is no job for the half-educated and the slovenly. Men and women doing capably whatever job is theirs to do tone up the whole society. And those who do a slovenly job, whether they are janitors or judges, surgeons or technicians, lower the tone of the society. So do the chiselers of high and low degree, the sleight-of-hand artists who always know how to gain an advantage without honest work. They are burdens on a free society.

But excellence implies more than competence. It implies a striving for the highest standards in every phase of life. We need individual excellence in all its forms—in every kind of creative endeavor, in politics, in education, in industry, in our spiritual life—in short, universally.

Those who are most deeply devoted to a democratic society must be precisely the ones who insist upon excellence, who insist that free men and women are capable of the highest standards of performance, who insist that a free society can be a great society in the richest sense of that phrase. The idea for which this nation stands will not survive if the highest goal free citizens can set themselves is an amiable mediocrity.

To the extent that we have achieved at least some of our worthiest aims as a nation, we have done so through fierce and faithful effort. Courageous men and women have spent lifetimes of struggle, endurance, and frustration in pursuit of those aims. Others have fought and died for them. And the same measure of devotion is required today. Unlike the great pyramids, the monuments of the spirit will not stand untended. They must be nourished in each generation by the allegiance of believing men and women. Free men and women, in their work, in their family life, and in their public behavior, should see themselves as builders and maintainers of the values of their society. Individual Americans—bus drivers and editors, grocers and senators, beauty parlor operators and ballplayers—can contribute to the greatness and strength of a free society, or they can help it to die.

It is easy for us to believe that freedom and justice are inexpensive commodities, always there, like the air we breathe, and not things we have to earn, be worthy of, fight for, and cherish. Nothing could be more dangerous to the future of our society. Free men and women must set their own goals. There is no one to tell them what to do; they must do it for themselves. They must be quick to apprehend the kinds of effort and performance their society needs, and they must demand that kind of effort and performance of themselves and of their fellows. They must cherish what Whitehead called "the habitual vision of greatness." If they have the wisdom and courage to demand much of themselves—as individuals and as a society—they may look forward to long-continued vitality. But a free society that is passive, inert, and preoccupied with its own diversions and comforts will not last long.

As Chesterton put it, "The world will never be safe for democracy—it is a dangerous trade."

But who ever supposed that it would be easy?

AFTERWORD

John W. Gardner: The Nation's Teacher

Whether we knew John W. Gardner as Mr. Secretary, Founder, Chairman, President, Author, Mentor, or Friend, he set our standard of excellence. His example, his deeds, his words are embedded, almost encoded, in our minds and hearts.

Most of us can probably recall at what stage in our lives we first read his books *Excellence* and *Self-Renewal* and how much we thought and talked about them—marking the pages and underlining thoughts and phrases we didn't want to take any chance we would ever forget.

How incredibly fortunate we are that he was *our* teacher, and *our* model. And how comforting it is to know that that has not ended.

On a far grander scale, with each book, monograph, and speech, imparting wisdom and hope he emerged as the *nation's* teacher, and that will *never* end.

His lessons were almost always friendly and encouraging, helping us to believe in ourselves; for example, in *Self-Renewal* he caught our attention thusly:

> There's something I know about you that you may not know about yourself. You have within you more resources of energy than have ever been tapped, more talent than has ever been exploited, more strength than has ever been tested, more to give than you have ever given.

229

For many of us John's lessons came as stories. What a treat and learning there was in just the everyday being with him as he reached into history and personal experience to impart a point and lock it into our minds forever.

For example, shortly after we had founded INDEPENDENT SECTOR I was asked to take a job that two years before I would have jumped at, but now the challenge John and I had entered into was just too fascinating and important to leave. When I told John of the offer and my decision, he told me a story.

In the earliest months of Common Cause, when the letters were just going out to solicit memberships, he was approached by Nelson Rockefeller, then governor of New York, to replace the slain Bobby Kennedy in the Senate. After momentary consideration, he explained to the governor that at another time he might have done it but "the situation was like that of the pole vaulter who had reached the top of his vault and had just let go of the pole, soaring toward the bar, his course and commitment unstoppable." Now *that's* a Gardner story. A riveting event, drama, action—and oh the imagery.

And there were different kinds of stories such as this one involving President Johnson:

> Many of LBJ's colorful—often earthy—expressions still linger in my mind. Once when we were under attack, he said, "John, sometimes you just have to hunker down like a jackass in a snowstorm." I had had such experiences but until then I hadn't known how to describe them.

John pointed out repeatedly to me that the Bible and its influence survived and spread because it tells the stories.

It will not surprise the reader to know that John, the communicator, was not impressed at all with today's fad of PowerPoint presentations.

Tell the stories, Brian. Tell the stories.

John's reputation spread so broadly and so deeply that people who didn't know him tended to assume that he was just a very serious fellow. He was serious but he was also wonderfully witty and just plain funny and fun. In his writings, speeches, and conversations he was always looking for humor to enliven the point, for example, this introduction to a commencement address:

> Thank you. I've always thought it prudent to savor the applause that comes *before* the speech. I remember the sign over the bar in Luckenbach, Texas that says, "If you're drinking to forget, please pay in advance."

John frequently slipped between the lines very funny thoughts and observations that you didn't see coming or weren't sure you'd heard correctly, and he'd be halfway into the next sentence before the laughter began to build, for example:

> Stupidity always surprises me but someone said the difference between genius and stupidity is that genius has its limits.

I've now gone over a lot of those speeches and checked the sentences following his subtle one-liners and they were just throwaways—just filler words until we caught on and caught up. I wish I'd known that earlier. I'd like to have confronted him that I had finally cracked the Gardner formula for comic "gotchas." It was equal parts of dry, wry, and sly.

John's lighter side involved much more than humor. He was just wonderfully good natured, warm, friendly, kind, civil—and that list could go on endlessly.

I can never think of the whole of the man Gardner without marveling at his rare combination of inquisitiveness, vision, pioneering, and leading.

He was all that and even more. All of us have our several additions; scholar, philosopher, historian, reformer, patriot, coalition builder, marine—all that too and even much more. On top of it all, he accomplished so staggeringly much but rarely made an enemy. His greatest adversaries were not individuals but indifference, apathy, and self-centeredness.

Despite all the honors and accomplishments, John remained a restless scholar, engaged in what he called "pushing the world."

Even toward the end he was teaching and pushing; for example, in his very last speech he ended with the following words:

I keep running into highly capable people all over this country who literally never give a thought to the well-being of their community. And I keep wondering who gave them permission to stand aside! I'm asking you to issue a wake-up call to those people—a bugle call right in their ear. And I want you to tell them that this nation could die of comfortable indifference to the problems that only citizens can solve. Tell them that.

He was and is telling all of us that what he described as "The American Experiment" is unfolding and fragile and that upholding the democratic compact is now all the more up to us.

This book provides one of the ways by which he will continue to teach and inspire us and those who come after us.

Brian O'Connell
Founding president of INDEPENDENT SECTOR
and professor of public service at the
University College of Citizenship and Public Service
at Tufts University

NOTES

All the selections were edited for inclusion in this book, many by John W. Gardner himself. The introductory text beneath each chapter head provides information on the original source material and credits where they are required.

Chapter 1. Glimpses of My Life

John W. Gardner selected this material from a variety of sources.

Chapter 2. In the President's Cabinet

This chapter is based on memoirs taped between 1992 and 2001, and on journals John W. Gardner kept at the time of the events described.

Chapter 3. Leading Common Cause

In 2001, John W. Gardner gathered this material together from prior writings, including extracts from *In Common Cause* (1972) and from speeches, incidental writings, and Common Cause materials.

Chapter 4. Personal Renewal

This piece began as a speech given to alumni of Stanford Graduate School of Business in 1986. It evolved and changed over the years. Gardner edited it one more time for this book.

Chapter 5. How to Tell When You've Grown Up

This essay is published here for the first time.

Chapter 6. The Fourth Maxim

This chapter originally appeared in the *Western Journal of Medicine*, July 1998.

Chapter 7. Touch the Earth

John W. Gardner gave this speech at the Kansas City Art Institute in 1975, on the occasion of receiving the first Thomas Hart Benton Award.

Chapter 8. The Qualities of Creativity

This chapter comes from *Self-Renewal*, Rev. ed. (New York: Norton, 1981), pp. 32–39. Copyright © 1981, 1964, 1963 by John W. Gardner. Used by permission of W.W. Norton & Company, Inc.

1. Vallery-Radot Pasteur, *Louis Pasteur: A Great Life in Brief* (New York: Knopf, 1958), pp. 84–85.

2. The discussion of creativity in this chapter draws heavily on the research of Frank Barron, Richard Crutchfield, Jacob Getzels, J. P. Guilford, Donald MacKinnon, Morris Stein and others. Creativity is an extraordinarily difficult and elusive research topic, and we owe a debt of gratitude to research workers who have had the courage and ingenuity to tackle it.

3. "Mozart's growth as a creator was like that of a rare and precious plant, whose innermost secret remains a mystery, but which is nourished by sun and rain and hindered by unfavorable weather." Alfred Einstein, *Mozart: His Character and His Work* (New York: Oxford University Press, 1945).

4. It is not surprising that there is overlap between the traits of the creative and of the self-renewing man. The psychological processes underlying creativity and self-renewal may prove to be very similar.

5. Donald W. MacKinnon, unpublished memorandum, November 1955, p. 14.

6. J. P. Guilford, "Creativity," *American Psychologist*, 5 (1950): 444–454.

7. Anne Roe, *The Making of a Scientist* (New York: Dodd, Mead, 1953).

Chapter 9. Commitment and Meaning

This chapter comes from *Self-Renewal*, Rev. ed. (New York: Norton, 1981), pp. 96–104. Copyright © 1981, 1964, 1963 by John W. Gardner. Used by permission of W.W. Norton & Company, Inc.

1. Gordon W. Allport, *Becoming* (New Haven, Conn.: Yale University Press, 1955), pp. 66–68.

2. M. E. Montaigne, *Essais*, edited by Maurice Rat (Paris: Classiques Garnier, 1962), Vol. II, p. 100. (Original work published 1588.)

3. Henry David Thoreau, *Walden and Civil Disobedience*, edited by Norman H. Pearson (Austin, Tex.: Holt, Rinehart and Winston, 1948), p. 55. (Original works published 1854 and 1849.)

4. Søren Kierkegaard, *Journal* (Aug. 1, 1835). In *A Kierkegaard Anthology*, edited by Robert Bretall (Princeton, N.J.: Princeton University Press, 1946), pp. 4–5.

5. Paul Tillich, *The Courage to Be* (New Haven, Conn.: Yale University Press, 1952), p. 47.

6. Erik H. Erikson, "The Problem of Ego Identity," *Journal of the American Psychoanalytical Association* 4, no. 1 (1956): 56.

7. Oliver Wendell Holmes, "The Law," speech given at the Suffolk Bar Association Dinner, Feb. 5, 1885, *Speeches* (New York: Little, Brown, 1913), p. 17.

Chapter 10. Motivation and the Triumphant Expression of Talent

This is a selection from chapter 16 of John W. Gardner's book *Excellence,* Rev. ed. (New York: Norton, 1984). Copyright © 1984, 1961 by John W. Gardner. Used by permission of W.W. Norton & Company, Inc.

1. Donald Day (ed.), *Uncle Sam's Uncle Josh* (New York: Little, Brown, 1953), p. 169.

Chapter 11. The Full Expression of Human Excellence

This chapter combines material from two editions of John W. Gardner's book *Excellence:* pp. xi–xiv from the first edition (New York: Harper & Row, 1961), and chapter 13 from the revised edition (New York: Norton, 1984).

1. G.W.E. Russell, *Collections and Recollections* (New York: Harper & Brothers, 1903).

2. Baltasar Gracian, *The Art of Worldly Wisdom,* translated by Joseph Jacobs (New York: Macmillan, 1892), p. 12. (Original work published 1647.)

Chapter 12. Our Moral and Spiritual Lineage

This is based on chapter 4 in *Morale* (New York: Norton, 1978). Copyright © 1978 by John W. Gardner. Used by permission of W.W. Norton & Company, Inc.

Chapter 13. The Nature of Leadership

This is chapter 1 in *On Leadership* (New York: Free Press, 1990). Reprinted with the permission of The Free Press, a division of Simon & Schuster Adult Publishing Group. Copyright © 1990 by John W. Gardner.

1. Niccolo Machiavelli, *The Prince* (New York: New American Library, 1952). (Original work published 1513.)

2. Sidney Hook, *The Hero in History* (Boston: Beacon Press, 1955).

3. Thomas E. Cronin, *Chronicle of Higher Education* (Feb. 1, 1989), pp. Bl-B2.

4. Jeffrey Pfeffer, "The Ambiguity of Leadership." In *Leadership: Where Else Can We Go?* edited by Morgan W. McCall Jr. and Michael Lombardo (Durham, N.C.: Duke University Press, 1978).

5. John W. Gardner, *Excellence,* Rev. ed. (New York: Norton, 1984).

Chapter 14. The Tasks of Leadership

This is chapter 2 in *On Leadership* (New York: Free Press, 1990). Reprinted with the permission of The Free Press, a division of Simon & Schuster Adult Publishing Group. Copyright © 1990 by John W. Gardner.

1. Philip Rieff, *The Triumph of the Therapeutic* (New York: HarperCollins, 1996).

2. Elisabeth Griffith, *In Her Own Right: The Life of Elizabeth Cady Stanton* (New York: Oxford University Press, 1984).

3. Jean Monnet, *Memoirs,* translated by Richard Mayne (New York: Doubleday, 1978).

4. Elspeth Huxley, *Florence Nightingale* (New York: Putnam, 1975).

5. Aaron Wildavsky, *The Nursing Father: Moses as a Political Leader* (Tuscaloosa: University of Alabama Press, 1984).

6. William Cabell Bruce, *John Randolph of Roanoke* (New York: Putnam, 1922).

7. Niccolo Machiavelli, *The Prince* (New York: New American Library 1952), p. 93. (Original work published 1513.)

8. Thurman Arnold, *The Folklore of Capitalism* (New Haven, Conn.: Yale University Press, 1937).

9. Rachel Carson, *Silent Spring* (New York: Houghton Mifflin, 1963).

10. Betty Friedan, *The Feminine Mystique* (New York: Dell, 1963).

11. Merrill D. Peterson, *The Jefferson Image in the American Mind* (New York: Oxford University Press, 1960).

12. Erik H. Erikson, *Gandhi's Truth* (New York: Norton, 1969); Mohandas D. Gandhi, *An Autobiography* (Boston: Beacon Press, 1957).

13. Monnet, *Memoirs,* p. 147.

14. Charles DeGaulle, *The War Memoirs, 1940–1946* (New York: Simon & Schuster, 1964), p. I:7.

15. Donald M. Michael, "Competence and Compassion in an Age of Uncertainty," *World Future Society Bulletin,* Jan.-Feb. 1983.

Chapter 15. The Heart of Leadership

This is chapter 3 in *On Leadership* (New York: Free Press, 1990). Reprinted with the permission of The Free Press, a division of Simon & Schuster Adult Publishing Group. Copyright © 1990 by John W. Gardner.

1. Max Weber, *The Theory of Social and Economic Organization,* translated by A. M. Henderson and Talcott Parsons (New York: Oxford University Press, 1947).

2. Georg Simmel, *The Sociology of Georg Simmel,* edited and translated by Kurt Wolff (Glencoe, Ill.: Free Press, 1950).

3. Excellent reviews of the research literature are available in B. M. Bass, *Stogdill's Handbook of Leadership* (New York: Free Press, 1981); B. M. Bass, *Leadership and Performance Beyond Expectations* (New York: Free Press, 1985); and Edwin Hollander, "Leadership and Power," in *The Handbook of Social Psychology*, 3d. ed., edited by G. Lindzey and E. Aronson (New York: Random House, 1985).

4. Woodrow Wilson, *Leaders of Men* (Princeton, N.J.: Princeton University Press, 1952), p. 43.

5. John F. Kennedy, *Profiles in Courage* (New York: Harper & Row, 1964), p. 134.

Chapter 16. The American Experiment

This chapter began as an essay. It was revised for a speech delivered to the Council for Excellence in Government in 1998, then extensively revised in subsequent years.

Chapter 17. Building Community

This chapter was originally published as a pamphlet of the same title by Independent Sector, 1991. Copyright © 1991 by John W. Gardner. Used with special permission of Independent Sector, Washington D.C., www.independentsector.org. It has been substantially shortened to fit the context of this book.

1. Robert A. Nisbet, *The Quest for Community* (Oxford, England: Oxford University Press, 1953).

2. Peter L. Berger and Richard John Neuhaus, *To Empower People: The Role of Mediating Structures in Public Policy* (Washington, D.C.: American Enterprise Institute, 1977).

3. Morris E. Eson and Eugene J. Webb, "The Role of Religion in Altruism and Philanthropy," Research Paper No. 1104, Graduate School of Business, Stanford University, 1991.

4. Los Angeles 2000 Committee, *LA 2000: A City for the Future*, 1988.

Chapter 18. Leading Community

The material in this chapter appeared in 1988 in "Leadership: An Overview," number 12 of a series titled *Leadership Papers* published by Independent Sector. Copyright © 1988 by John W. Gardner. Used with special permission of Independent Sector, Washington D.C., www.independentsector.org. It has been edited extensively.

1. "Community-Based Development: Investing in Renewal." Report of the Task Force on Community-Based Development, Sept. 1987, p. 35.

2. Kenneth Benne and Paul Sheats, "Functional Roles of Group Members," *Journal of Social Issues* 2 (1948): 41–49.

3. Alex Bavelas, "Leadership: Man and Function," *Administrative Science Quarterly* (March 1960).

4. Edgar H. Schein, *Organizational Psychology* (Upper Saddle River, N.J.: Prentice Hall, 1980), p. 251.

Chapter 19. The Independent Sector

This piece is from the Foreword to Brian O'Connell, *America's Voluntary Spirit* (New York: Foundation Center, 1983). Copyright © 1983. Used by permission of The Foundation Center, 79 Fifth Avenue, New York, N.Y. 10003. http://fdncenter.org.

Chapter 20. The American Dream

This essay originally appeared in IBM's *THINK Magazine* in 1976.

Chapter 21. Freedom and Obligation, Liberty and Duty

This is chapter 17, originally titled "The Aims of a Free People," from John W. Gardner's book *Excellence*, Rev. ed. (New York: Norton, 1984). Copyright © 1984, 1961 by John W. Gardner. Used by permission of W.W. Norton & Company, Inc.

1. Thomas Huxley, "On Medical Education," from *Science and Education: Essays* (New York: Appleton, 1896).

2. Alfred North Whitehead, preface to Wallace B. Donham, *Business Adrift* (New York: McGraw-Hill, 1931).

3. William Hazlitt, *Lectures on the English Comic Writers* (London: Carey, 1819).

INDEX

A

Accountability: of leaders, 201–202; systems ensuring, 202–203
Adams, John, 150
Advocacy, 171
Agenda setting, as task of leadership, 132–133
Aging: anecdotes about, 8–9; and commitment, 49, 221; and renewal, 42–43, 51
Alexander the Great, 67
Allport, Gordon W., 77
America: evolution of, 105–106; as political experiment, xxvi, 159–161, 172–173; shared vision of, 103–104, 108
American Dream, 213–217
American Leadership Forum, 187
Antaeus, 62
Anthony, Susan B., 160
Arnold, Thurman, 135
Authority, official, of leaders, 115–116

B

Bailey, Thomas, 5
Baker, Bobby, 25
Bannister, Roger, 89
Bavelas, Alex, 198
Behrman, S. N., 45
Benne, Kenneth, 198
Benton, Thomas Hart, 61
Berger, Peter L., 176
Berra, Yogi, 43
Blair, Charlie, 3
Bolívar, Simón, 129
Bolton, Herbert, 7
Bolton, Thaddeus, 7

Bonding experiences, 180, 185
Boredom, 42
Building Community (Gardner), xxv
Bureaucracy: in Washington, D.C., 18–19; White House as, 23
Burke, Edmund, 150
Bush, George Sr., 134
Business, leaders in, 144

C

Caesar, Julius, 114
Califano, Joseph, xiv, 23, 26
California history, Gardner's interest in, 7
Campaign financing, regulations on, 32–33
Carlyle, Thomas, 120
Carnegie, Andrew, 160
Carnegie Corporation, xxii–xxiii, 12
Carson, Rachel, 136
Carter, Jimmy, xxv
Cervantes, 50
Charitable giving, by individual citizens, 207–208
Chavez, Cesar, 160
Chesterton, Gilbert Keith, 227
Children: living up to expectations, 87–89; surroundings of, and identity, 62–64
Churchill, Winston, 118, 123; on difficulties ahead, 49, 89; as example of renewal, 50; historical context of, 120
Citizens: charitable giving by, 207–208; holding leaders accountable, 201–203; involvement by, 163–164, 165, 171–172; lobbying group for, 31,

36–37; organizations of, 197–198; participation by, 186–187, 196–197; sharing leadership tasks, 198–201

Civil rights legislation, 21, 24

Civilization: factors contributing to rise of, 88; as shared vision, 103–104, 129, 168. *See also* Society

Cohen, Wilbur, 21–22

Collaboration, in community building, 166–167

Commitment: American, 76; Americans' desire for, 220–221; to heal society, 168–169; meaning derived from, 47–49, 81–82; mutual, 55

Common Cause, xxiv, 29–37; and campaign financing regulations, 32–33; as citizens' lobbying group, 31, 36–37; early mail to, 30; and enforcement of disclosure laws, 35–36; reform of state laws championed by, 35, 36; and secrecy in government, 34–35

Communication: in communities, 185–186; between leaders and followers, 147–149

Communities: affirmation in, 187–188; attributes of, 181–191; building and rebuilding, 162–163, 166–167, 180–181; caring and teamwork in, 184–185; communication in, 185–186; contemporary forms of, 179–180; disintegration of, 161–162, 177, 180, 210; disregard for well-being of, 232; diversity in, 163, 166–167, 181–182; educational component of, 189; future as viewed by, 189–190; government of, 190–191; institutions for maintaining, 190–191; leadership of, 175, 195–203; links to outside, 188–189; as necessary for free society, 175–176, 191–193; participation in, 186–187, 196–197; religious, 169; shared values of, 175–176, 183; traditional, 178

Conant, James B., 99

Conflict resolution, 167–168, 184–185

Confucius, 97

Congress, Gardner's experience with, 19–23

Constituents. *See* Followers

Creativity, 65–71; fostering, 67, 234n4; prevalence of, 66–67; traits associated with, 68–71, 86

Cronin, Thomas, 121

Culture: and leader-follower relationship, 146; shared, of leaders and followers, 149. *See also* Diversity; Pluralism

Curley, James, 149

D

Decision making, as task of leadership, 132

Deer, Ada, 160

DeGaulle, Charles, 138–139, 147

Delta Foundation, 198

Dent, Charles W., Congressman, 34

Department of Health, Education, and Welfare (HEW): and Congress, 19–23; Gardner as Secretary of, xxiii–xxiv, 11–28; and Johnson administration, 23–27; leadership of, 13–17; "theater" of, 12–13, 28; and Washington bureaucracy, 18–19

Devolution, 165–166

Dickinson, Emily, 98

Dillard, Annie, 52

Diogenes, 67

Diversity: and community building, 163, 166–167; wholeness incorporating, 133–134, 181–182. *See also* Pluralism

Dole, Elizabeth Hanford, 134

Dole, Robert, 134

Don Quixote (Cervantes), 50

Douglas, Norman, 45

Dukakis, Michael, 134

Duke of Wellington, 95

E

Earth, relationship to, and identity, 62–64

Ecclesiastes, 106–107

Echohawk, John, 160

Education: as component of communities, 189; liberal, value of, 5

Einstein, Albert, 127

Eisenhower, Dwight, 118

Elite, leaders as, 116

Emerson, Ralph Waldo, xvi

Empowerment, as task of leadership, 139–140

Enabling, as task of leadership, 139–140

Enthusiasm, 90

Equality, unexamined aspects of, 93–94

Erikson, Erik H., 81

Ervin, Sam, 21

Excellence: Can We Be Equal and Excellent Too? (Gardner), xxiii

Excellence: individual conceptions of, 94–95; kinds of, 95–98; needed throughout society, 98–101; pursuit of, in free society, 225–227

Expectations: and faith in people, 89–91; as motivator, 87–89

Experience, finding order in, 70–71

Explaining, as task of leadership, 135–136

F

Failures: as inevitable part of life, 56; learning from, 44, 45

Faith: civic, loss of, 164; in people, and expectations, 89–91

Families: necessity of preserving, 162–163; shared values of, 175–176. *See also* Communities

Farmer, Larry, 198

Fatalism, passivity linked to, 86

Feminine Mystique (Friedan), 136

"Fire fighting," 18

Flexibility, of creative people, 69–70

Fogerty, John, 20

Followers: communication between leaders and, 147–149; hidden desires and emotions of, 154; interaction between leaders and, 114, 131, 143–155, 198–199; strengthening, 153–155; trust in leaders, 152–153

Francis, Saint, 97

Franklin, Benjamin, 172

Free society: multiple meanings/goals acceptable in, 81–83; necessity of communities for, 175–176, 191–193; obligations necessary in, 192, 219–220; pursuit of excellence in, 225–227; young people needed by, 223–224. *See also* Society

Friedan, Betty, 136, 160

Future, impossibility of foretelling, 104–105

G

Galileo, 65–66

Gandhi, Mohandas, 117, 118, 137

Gardner, John W.: biography of, xxi–xxvi, 3–9; books written by, xxiii, xxiv–xxv, xxvi; at Carnegie Corporation, xxii–xxiii, 12; childhood of, xxi, 3–4; as college student, xxi, 4–5; Common Cause founded by, xxiv, 29–37; INDEPENDENT SECTOR founded by, xxv, 205; journaling by, xvii–xviii; marriage of, xxi, 5–6; reading and self-education by, 7; relationship with LBJ, xiv–xv, 23–27; as Secretary of HEW, xxiii–xxiv, 11–28; storytelling by, 230–231; teaching by, xxii, 8, 229–232

Garmatz, Eddie, 32

Goals: envisioning, as task of leadership, 127–129, 139; multiple, in free society, 82–83; striving toward, 77–78

Golden, Harry, 58

Gompers, Samuel, 160

Government: charitable giving fostered by, 207; community, 190–191; devolution in, 165–166; ensuring accountability of, 202–203; public opinion of, 166

Gracian, Baltasar, 97

Growing up: criteria for assessing progress in, 55–56; length of process of, 44

Guilford, J. P., 69

H

Hamilton, Alexander, 160

Happiness, contemporary vs. realistic conception of, 75–77, 221

Harris, La Donna, 160

Hays, Wayne, 36

Hazlitt, William, 225

Hegel, Georg, 120

Hobbes, Thomas, 153

Holmes, Oliver Wendell, 83

Hook, Sidney, 120

Hope: as basic human motivator, 85–86; kept alive by leaders, 85, 127, 131

Houston, Sam, 150–151
Human resources. *See* Talent
Humphrey, Hubert, 25
Huxley, Thomas, 224

I

Ideals, striving toward, xxiv, 107–108
Identity, childhood/youth roots as element of, 62–64. *See also* Meaning
In Common Cause (Gardner), xxiv
Independence, of creative people, 68–69
INDEPENDENT SECTOR, xxv, 205
Independent sector. *See* Nonprofit sector
Institutions: building, as task of leadership, 132; future, 104–105; for maintenance of community, 190–191
Iran-Contra affair, 137
Isabella, Queen of Spain, 120

J

Jackson, Jesse, 134
Jacobi, C.G.J., 225
James, William, 75, 89
Javits, Jacob, 19
Jefferson, Thomas, 117, 160, 172; historical context of, 119; on institutions ensuring accountability, 202; as symbol, 136–137
Jesus, 98, 130
John XXIII, Pope, 50
Johnson, Lyndon (LBJ): colorful expressions of, 18, 230; comment on Gardner, xiv; decided not to seek re-election, xv, 26–27; political knowledge of, 24–25; priority setting by, 131–132; working with, as Secretary of HEW, xiv–xv, xxiii–xxiv, 23–27
Jonsson, Erik, 200
Jouvenel, Bertrand de, 154

K

Kamp, Jack, 134
Keneally, Connie, 34
Kennedy, John F., xxiii, 136
Kennedy, Robert, 230
Kepler, Johannes, 98
Kierkegaard, Søren, 81
King, Coretta Scott, 134
King, Martin Luther Jr., 86, 160

L

Leaders: accountability of, 201–203; communication between followers and, 147–149; expectations of, 87–89; with faith in human possibility, 89–91; and history, 114, 119–120, 122–123; hope kept alive by, 85, 127, 131; interaction between followers and, 114, 131, 143–155, 198–199; judgments of, 122–123; kinds of, 118–119; managers as, 116–118; political, 144, 150–153; and power, 115; response to pluralism, 151–152; settings for, 114, 121; and status, 115; as symbols, 15–17, 136–137, 139; trust in, 152–153, 161
Leadership: of communities, 175, 195–203; context for, 114, 119–121; defined, 113; of Department of HEW, 13–17; institutionalizing, 124–125; need for dispersed, 121, 123–124; qualities/positions mistaken for, 115–116; sharing tasks of, 198–201; symbolic nature of, 15–17; tasks of, 127–141; teaching as integral to, 8, 135–136
Learning: discontinuing, 41–43; lifelong, 82; in maturity, 43–46, 51; risk involved in, 46
Lee, Russell, 59
Leonidas, 97
Lincoln, Abraham, 90, 97–98, 123, 136, 160
Long, Huey, 93
Long, Russell, 22–23
Louis, Joe, 45
Luther, Martin, 120

M

MacArthur, Douglas, 118
Machiavelli, N., 114, 135
MacKinnon, Donald, 68, 70
Madison, James, 160
Management, as task of leadership, 14, 131–133
Managers, as leaders, 116–118
Marroquin, Aida, marriage to, xxi, 5–6
Marshall, George, 118
Marshall, Thurgood, 160

Marx, Karl, 120
Maturity: criteria for assessing, 55–56; time required to reach, 44
Maxims: brevity of, 57–58; one-word, 58–60; on relationship to Earth, 62
Meaning: beyond satisfying needs, 78–79; derived from commitment, 47–49, 81–82; human hunger for, 80–81; individual construction of, xiii, 53; multiple, acceptable in free society, 81–82
Media: aided formation of Common Cause, 30; image of leaders constructed in, 153
Michael, Donald, 141
Middleton, Harry, xv
Mississippi Action for Community Education (MACE), 198
Monnet, Jean, 132, 134, 138–139
Montaigne, M. E., 78, 96
Montesquieu, 220
Montgomery, Bernard, 118
Morale (Gardner), xxv
Morris, Robert, 172
Motivation: and attitude toward future, 49; from commitment, 47–49; expectations as, 87–89; and faith in human possibilities, 89–91; and hope, 85–86; as task of leadership, 130–131; Utopianism as obstacle to, 86–87
Mozart, Wolfgang Amadeus, 98, 234n3

N

The National Association for Community Leadership, 187
National Renewal (Gardner), xxvi
National Urban Coalition, xxiv, 208
Neuhaus, John, 176
Newman, Cardinal, 106
Nightingale, Florence, 98, 118, 133
Nisbet, Robert, 176
Nixon, Richard, 24, 35
No Easy Victories (Gardner), xxiv
Nonprofit sector, 205–211; attributes of, 209–211; charitable giving enabling, 207–208; pluralism of, 209, 211; role of, 206–207
The Nursing Father: Moses as a Political Leader (Wildavsky), 133

O

Obligations, required for freedom, 192, 219–220
O'Connell, Brian, xvii, xxv, 205
On Leadership (Gardner), xxv
Openness, of creative people, 68
Optimism, tough-minded, 49
Organizational Psychology (Schein), 198–199
Organizations, citizen, 197–198

P

Paine, Thomas, 136
Participation, in communities, 186–187, 196–197
Pasteur, Louis, 66
Pastori, John, 21–22
Patton, George, 118
Perkins, Carl, 20
Peterson, Merrill, 137
Pfeffer, Jeffrey, 122
Pluralism: leaders' response to, 151–152; of nonprofit sector, 209, 211. *See also* Diversity
Politics: leaders in, 144, 150–153; necessity of, 32; as task of leadership, 133
Power: accountability of holders of, 201–203; and leaders, 115
Priority setting, as task of leadership, 131–132
Proverbs: brevity of, 57–58; one-word, 58–60; on relationship to Earth, 62

Q

Quotations of Wit and Wisdom (Gardner), xxiv, 57

R

Randolph, John, 134
Reagan, Ronald, xxv, 123
Renewal: examples of, 50–51; fostering, as task of leadership, 117, 139; personal, need for, 41–53; processes fostering creativity and, 234n4; striving toward goals as element of, 77–78
Representation, as task of leadership, 138–139
Richards, Dick, 52–53
Rieff, Philip, 129

Risk taking: by creative people, 69; by leaders, 145; with learning, 46
Rockefeller, Nelson, 230
Roe, Anne, 71
Roosevelt, Franklin Delano, 6, 106, 122
Russell, Richard, 21, 25
Ruth, 98

S

Schein, Edgar H., 198–199
Schweitzer, Albert, 137
Secrecy in government, Common Cause's lobbying against, 34–35
Self-doubt, 96
Self-Renewal (Gardner), xxiii, 16
Shackleton, Ernest, 52
Shannon, Jim, 19
Shaw, George Bernard, 192, 206
Shaw, H. W., 88
Sheats, Paul, 198
Shriver, Sargent, xiv
Silent Spring (Carson), 136
Simmel, Georg, 144
Sloan, Alfred, 132
Smith, Logan Pearsall, 42
Social problems: complexity of solving, 27, 78; innovative ways of solving, 164–165
Society: change in attitude toward talent in, 98; as constantly in decay, 103; evolution of, 105–108; influence of individual behavior in, 108–109; need for excellence throughout, 98–101. *See also* Civilization; Free society
Spencer, Herbert, 120
Stanford University, xxi, xxv, 4–5
Stanton, Elizabeth Cady, 128–129, 130, 160
Status, and leaders, 115
Stevenson, Robert Louis, 47
Symbols, leaders as, 15–17, 136–137, 139

T

Talent: motivating expression of, 85–91; society's change in attitude toward, 98; undeveloped, 140
Teachers: expectations of, 87–89; faith of, in human possibility, 89–91

Teaching: as Gardner's life work, xxii, 8, 229–232; as integral to leadership, 8, 135–136
Texas, "open government" reform legislation in, 35
Thoreau, Henry David, 79
Tillich, Paul, 81
Trust: in communities, 184–185; in leaders, 152–153, 161; preservation of, as task of leadership, 134–135

U

Unification, as task of leadership, 133–134
Utopianism, as obstacle to motivation, 86–87

V

Values: actions as embodying, 108–109, 169–171; affirming and regenerating, as tasks of leadership, 129–130; shared by Americans, 222–223; shared in communities, 175–176, 183
Vision, shared: of America, 103–104, 108; civilization as, 103–104, 129, 168
Volunteering, value of, 171

W

Ward, Artemus, 79
Washington, D.C.: bureaucracy in, 18–19; history of, 11–12; working with strong people in, 13–15, 20–22
Washington, George, 134, 172
Weber, Max, 144
Whitaker, Jim, 44
Whitehead, Alfred North, 224, 226
Whitney, Eli, 98
Wildavsky, Aaron, 133
Wilson, Woodrow, 145, 148
Work, meaning derived from, 48
Wright, Frank Lloyd, 122

Y

Young people, free society's need for, 223–224